Carol Duncombe was born to Frank and Babs in Northampton. She has four siblings – two brothers and two sisters. She started her nursing career when she was 18. She has worked as a midwife for 45 years and delivered over 2000 babies. She retired last year and now spends her time helping out at a local school. She's been married to Richard for 45 years.

Love

Carol Jaude.

Dedication

I dedicate this book to my husband, Richard; my daughters,
Charlotte and Emma; and their partners, Justin and John; and my
gorgeous grandchildren, twins Edward and George, and Evee; and
all my lovely ladies at Olney.

Carol Duncombe

A MIDWIFE'S MEMOIRS

AUSTIN MACAULEY PUBLISHERS™

LONDON • CAMBRIDGE • NEW YORK • SHARJAH

A CIP catalogue record for this title is available from the British Library.

ISBN 9781788789622 (Paperback)
ISBN 9781788789639 (Hardback)
ISBN 9781788789646 (E-Book)

www.austinmacauley.com

First Published (2018)
Austin Macauley Publishers Ltd™
25 Canada Square
Canary Wharf
London
E14 5LQ

Acknowledgements

Thanks to the Balney Charity Trust for their support and to Becky and Gill for encouraging me to write my book.

I was a third-year midwifery student attending my first home birth alone. My midwife mentor had rung me, said, "Go, get on with it and ring me when she is near to delivering." Oh my goodness, it was the middle of the night, also I had no transport, so I duly called a taxi as instructed and off I went.

I was terrified but I arrived at the house and met a lovely lady and her husband who were very kind to me. I examined her and thought, *This seems to be a small baby. I can find limbs all over the place – not a good place to be in.* So, I asked the lady how and where the baby was moving, to try and ascertain the position. I really had no idea. I duly did the usual checks and found her to be 8cm dilated (the cervix needs to be 10cm to deliver baby), so I phoned my midwife and told her the birth would be imminent, and I thought it was a small baby.

I heard her tut and thought, *Oh flip, she thinks I am useless,* but she told me she would be right along. An hour later, she had still not arrived and the woman started to push. My stress levels were very high when the door knocked and in came my saviour. She sat in the corner and watched and I duly delivered quite a small baby. At which point, the midwife leapt to her feet, palpated the woman's abdomen and said, "Anyone told you? You are having twins." I don't know who was most shocked, me or the parents; but the 2nd baby arrived and we all breathed a sigh of relief. "Well done," said my mentor, "you were right about one thing, there were a lot of limbs. Now clear up, get yourself back to the nurse's home, you are back on duty in 4 hrs."

And so, my career as a midwife had begun.

How it all began.

Chapter 1

I was an 18-year-old going to an interview for nursing with my mum! We arrived at Northampton hospital on the bus and were invited into the matron's office. The matron was a very posh lady, very upright and extremely smart in her uniform. She had a cut-glass accent. I remember being asked questions about why I wanted to enter nursing and giving some incoherent replies. After several minutes, the matron excused herself and Mum and I looked at each other and burst out laughing. We were completely hysterical, it was a good job she was out of the room for several minutes so we could compose ourselves.

We were taken on a tour of the hospital and noticed how the nurses tried to disappear when the matron approached the wards. It was evident that the matron ruled the roost and ward sisters rolled down their sleeves before speaking to her.

We were taken into the school of nursing above, which was three floors of rooms; where the nurses lived – everyone had to live there; there was no living at home and commuting. The top floor was for the night nurses so they were not disturbed during the day.

That was my interview. Several days later, I received a letter telling me to report to the school of nursing on September 1; to start my training. I was given a list of items which I should take with me. This included black, flat, lace-up shoes, black tights with seam down back of leg, notebooks, pens and pencils, and a black cardigan.

September 1 arrived and so did I at the nurse's home, apprehensive and feeling a bit alone. I had always lived at home and the thought of living away from family and friends was daunting.

The Beginning of My Training

The first day involved getting our uniforms: Blue and white striped dress, white press stud collar, white belt and white starched apron. The belt showed how green we all were, 1st years wore white, 2nd years wore white with blue stripe and 3rd years wore a blue belt. We put on our stockings and black lace-up shoes, and then came the hat: a starched piece of material which had to be moulded to the shape needed and kept on our head with Kirby grips; hair had to be off the shoulder and smart. The best part of the uniform was the cape, black lined with red extremely smart and warm for walking around the hospital complex.

As very junior nurses, we were known by our surnames; I was Nurse Thorpe and knew other nurses by their surname. We were not allowed to use our Christian names; and if caught using them would be reprimanded. Then we had the scarf, an optional extra we were allowed to wear. We were so proud to wear this. They were only worn by Northampton nurses and could only be bought at a specialist shop close to the hospital. I remember being out in my work clothes black coat and scarf when I was a very junior nurse. I came upon a car accident. I whipped off my scarf and shoved it inside my coat. I was still in the first weeks of my training so thought I would be a liability rather than a help. But, I still remember it and feel a bit uncomfortable about doing it.

Lights out was at 10pm and until that time several of us got together for a chin wag and cup of tea. We were informed that breakfast was at 7.30am and we should be fully dressed in our uniform. Once we had finished, we should be ready to start in school at 9am. Meals were in the canteen and we formed an orderly queue and waited to be served. There was a pecking order in the canteen and if a staff nurse or senior nurse was behind you, it was etiquette to let them go ahead of you. Many times, we spent a lot of time going from the front to the back of the queue and getting served 5 mins before we needed to be back on duty. We learned to eat very quickly.

Nursing school was frightening: we learnt how to take blood pressures, temperatures and there was a life size doll called Dolly; who we practiced our skills on. We bed bathed, talked to and shaved Dolly, passed tubes, stuck needles in her. All being watched over by senior tutors who scared us to death. One rule I could not get my head around was when taking temperatures, we had to shake the thermometer, which was made of glass, down. Before wiping it in a chemical and putting it in the patient's mouth or other orifice if this was not right for the patient. When shaking these glass thermometers, a number of us sent them flying into the atmosphere – apparently if this happened when we reached the wards, we were reported to the matron and the cost of it was taken out of our pay packet!!!

Pre-nursing school lasted for six weeks after which we had to go to the ward accompanied by a tutor and perform a procedure on a real patient. I had to take a temperature and blood pressure whilst talking to the patient. This was multitasking on a big scale for me at this point. Fortunately, I got through it and so passed on to the next step of my career. Some of my new friends were not so lucky. One girl had to give two glycerine suppositories to a patient. She handed them to her on a plate with a knife and fork. We never saw her again, I cannot think why!

Chapter 2
Life on the Wards

Life on the wards was hard, rules had to be adhered to and Sister on the ward was God to us. The hours were long, and we spent many hours massaging our feet in our off time. I remember one Sister; she was very Irish and liked all the nurses who were Catholics. She gave them time off for mass, the rest of us lesser mortals kept the ward going until they returned. This was usually in the sluice washing used bed pans, none of your disposables in those days. The bedpan round was done on a regular basis and God help any patient who needed to relieve themselves between these times. This Sister terrified me, but strangely enough at the end of my training she asked me back as her staff nurse and I worked with her for 2 years and loved it and her.

When I was in my first year as a staff nurse, I was taken ill with Appendicitis and landed as a patient on this very ward. Sister arrived at 7.30am the next morning, to tell me I had mucked up her off-duty plans. It all had to be changed now I was off. I remember being very apologetic. A few days later, I had a rigor (shaking uncontrollably), due to a high temperature. All I can remember of this is the Sister coming to the bed and rolling up her sleeves. This was a sign a patient was very ill and it terrified me; but she was extremely kind and showed me her true colours. She was actually a pussy cat who was there for her patients and would do anything for them. She taught me what caring was and I have never forgotten her.

On my first ward, I was with another student when we were informed that a patient had died. As neither of us had seen a body before, we were invited to go into the side room and view the gentlemen. We took a deep breath, walked in together and slowly pulled back the sheet. At that moment, we saw his arm move, we both ran from the room in total shock and disbelief. The sister was there saying you need to get used to looking after the dead. When we stuttered out that he wasn't dead, he had moved, she shot into the room and sure enough he was alive. This gentleman actually recovered and went home a few weeks later. It took us longer than that to get over the shock. Apparently, a junior doctor had declared the man deceased. He was made to apologize to us. We actually felt sorry for him he was so upset. I bet he never made that mistake again.

On one of my first wards, I was asked by the sister to go to see an elderly gentleman who was in a side room. He was having problems with leaking urine. To help with this problem he was to have a soft piece of tubing put over his penis. Well into the side ward I went, I had an awful problem getting the tubing in the right place. I remember well going out to the sister and saying, "I cannot get it on, it keeps swelling."

She said, "leave it to me I will do it."

I was so naïve at the time I was 18 and had not got the foggiest idea what an erection was. I bet the sister had a great laugh about it. For ages, I never understood what had happened. Oops, how green I was, but I was not the only one, my fellow student nurses were in the same position. I had had a very sheltered upbringing and although I had brothers, men were a bit of a mystery to me at the time.

I remember one day a group of about eight students were invited to see a fairly young chap have a catheter inserted into his bladder. We all stood round whilst this poor man looked so embarrassed. It was not long until we were all asked to leave as his body did what any man would do in front of young girls. This is really appalling and would never be allowed to happen these days.

Chapter 3
Night Duty

Night duty was another hill to climb. There were no sisters or staff nurses on the wards, the wards were run by students. A sister came to each ward between 9pm and 10pm and did the drug round. We were expected to know the diagnosis of each patient. I remember one sister, who at the end of the round, commented, "You have a lot of men with prostate problems tonight! When you couldn't remember a diagnosis, you had a guess."

One of the most senior sisters who came to do the rounds was a large lady, very kind, but suffered from wind. All the way around the ward she farted, I was too scared to laugh. But, after she had left the ward it caused a lot of humour. One of the patients commented that she should join a brass band. Unfortunately, he thought she was a bit off key.

At night, it was an ideal opportunity to get to know your patients, as there were no doctors' rounds, or visitors coming in. We could sit with patients who couldn't sleep and talk to them or make them a cup of tea. I well remember one old chap on the male medical ward. He was in his nineties and loved chatting to the nurses. He wore a bed cap to sleep and loved to be tucked in and kissed goodnight. He was a darling and all the nurses loved him. One night I was kissing him goodnight, when the sister arrived to do her round. I heard her bellow up the ward, do you kiss all every patient goodnight. This little old man yelled back. No, only me. Bless him; we were quite sad when he went home.

One thing I couldn't understand was when the sister arrived to do the drug round, this was supposed to be between 8 pm and 10pm, but as she had a lot of wards to cover she was sometimes late than this. We would go from bed to bed checking which medication the patient needed. A lot of the time, the patients were asleep. We would wake them up to ask if they wanted a sleeping tablet. This always seemed bizarre to me but as most patients were written up for sleeping pills in those days, I suppose she thought that if they woke up and asked for their medication and the sister had done her round, they would not be able to get it.

Challenging Times

One ward that was a bit of a challenge for me was the Ear, Nose and Throat ward on tonsillectomy surgery days. There would be up to about 12 children who had been to theatre and they would all be nursed in one big ward. Nurses went from bed to bed trying to comfort the children. It is so much better these days when parents can stay with their children to help to comfort them after their surgery.

Tonsils are not taken out now as they were when I was a student nurse which can only be a good thing. My daughters have both had their tonsils out. Charlotte was first and her operation went well. Emma was only 18 months old when she had the operation. She had been ill with tonsil infections many times, also ear infections, so it was good that this would hopefully put an end to her infections.

I recall after having the operation, the consultant came to see her. He told us that her tonsils were enormous, her adenoids were huge and the muck that came out of her ears was incredible. I was feeling shock at the time as the nurse had just been around to ask what she would like for her breakfast. She wanted toast; and ate it without a problem. The consultant said she has had a sore throat for so long. This must be a normal thing for her. We had fed Charlotte lots of ice cream after her operation. Emma just ate normally and never looked back.

Working on the Children's ward was lovely, but parents were only allowed to visit during the allotted hours. I remember it was between 2 and 4 in the afternoon. It was a lovely ward with a great sister who cared so much about her patients. We did a daily sweet round. This was obviously something that the children looked forward to. It was the highlight of their day.

Night duty on the Children's ward was always difficult. Children always cry for their parents when they cannot sleep, or are feeling unwell, it was difficult to try to comfort these children. The only concession was that we could eat the Farley's rusks, and eat the stash of sweets in the middle of the night. They were yummy at the time and helped to keep us going. There were only two of us on duty at night, and we were always relieved when the day staff arrived.

Most of the children were kept in bed, especially if they had had surgery. Trying to keep young children in their beds when all they wanted to do was to go home was not easy. There were no play specialists or other helpers to assist with this. The worst time was when visiting ended. Obviously, all the children were upset when their parents went home and we were left to pick up the pieces. We tried our best, cuddling, consoling and doing what we could to comfort them. Thank goodness soon after this time parents were allowed to stay with their children throughout the day, so life became much easier for the children and for the staff.

Old Buildings

One of the wards was a Nissen hut built during the war. It was well known for having cockroaches in residence. At night, you could see and hear them marching up the ward. It was not nice and kept us moving to keep out of their way. This was one of the first wards I worked on. It was male medical, I remember on one occasion the Mayor of Northampton was visiting.

It was a long nightingale ward and the first man inside the door had a form of dementia. He was extremely sweet and loving, but if he wasn't in the mood to cooperate everyone knew about it. He decided this was one occasion that wasn't to his liking, and to show his annoyance as the mayor walked up the ward he was throwing little balls of what we thought was rubbish at him and his entourage. We found out later it was poo. It was extremely comical but the sister was not happy and gave us all a lecture on decorum.

We were paid a wage whilst we were students. I remember my pay was £13 for a month. This was low but we managed to save and buy what we needed as we did not pay for board or lodgings. We had a lot of fun in the nursing home. We were often a bit short of cash, so tried to save money whenever we could. In the laundry room, we had washing machines and mangles. If we were short of toothpaste, we would put the tube through the mangle, it kept us going for a few more days. The toilets were in a row, and if a friend was in the next cubicle we would stand on the loo seat and flush the chain whilst they were doing their business, sounds very childish now but it amused us at the time.

My Pet Hate

One of my pet hates when I was a student was working in Theatre. It freaked me out, especially the Ophthalmic Theatre (eyes). The sister in charge of the eye ward could see my distress and was very kind. She let me work on the ward as much as possible, but I had to venture into the dreaded theatre too often for my comfort.

When I moved to general theatres, I was not quite so lucky. I had to do my stint and just suck it up. I remember being in theatre one day with a good friend of mine who was also a student. The surgeon was elderly and grumpy. He was doing a bowel operation on the patient. It was long operation and at one point we were giggling over some little thing. A swab that had been finished with had been thrown and it had gone down my friend's theatre boots; and I was fishing it out of her boot with long handed forceps. Then I heard, "Catch that," and I put my hand out and he threw a scalpel at me. It cut all my fingers, not badly but enough to bleed quite profusely. It sounds shocking, and certainly wouldn't be allowed these days, but in those days, surgeons were demi gods and whatever they did was accepted.

Accident and Emergency

I loved working in Accident and Emergency it was much calmer than it seems to be these days. All the patients who visited the apartment were in need of sutures, plastering to their limbs, or perhaps were having an asthma attack. The staff worked together, were a good team and days and nights passed quickly. You learnt a lot and also saw things that were sometimes quite shocking.

I remember being on duty one night when a young motor cyclist was brought in after crashing into a tree. He was rushed to theatre, I was asked to stand at the end of the bed. The surgeon proceeded to amputate his leg and then gave it to me. It is the only time I ever fainted, and I still remember it to this day.

I also remember a cricketer coming in after being hit in the temple with a cricket ball. He was deeply unconscious and remained so for almost a week. I heard later that he had responded to treatment and had gone home about a month later. Thank goodness cricketers wear helmets these days when facing that hard ball.

A lot of the night, if we were not busy, we would spend on making up packs for the day staff. Also, cleaning cupboards and equipment so that it was ready when needed. I don't think staff would have time to do this in the current climate. I cannot remember any patients coming into the department having drunk too much or have taken illegal drugs. How times change.

Chapter 4
Into the 2nd Year of Training

As we progressed through training we were given more and more responsibility. As 2nd year students were expected to run the wards when the sister or staff nurse was not available. It was really frightening. We were expected to do ward rounds with the doctors, who were gods in those days, some really enjoyed making you look small.

On one occasion a first-year student had been asked to shorten a drain that had been put in a patient wound. The doctor had ordered this, and the nurse said she was happy to do this task.

At the end of the round, the doctors returned to the ladies' bedside and when looking at the wound asked where the drain was. The nurse told him she had done as he asked and shortened it. Unfortunately, she had not replaced the pin that would have stopped the drain slipping inside the patient. This poor lady had to go to theatre to have the drain removed from inside her wound. I felt really sorry for the nurse involved but we all had to learn harsh lessons and this definitely was one.

One of the things I really hated was a job that had to be done on male medical. We had a lot of older men who came in with chest problems. They were encouraged to cough up what was on their chests. This was good for them but bad for the students. They were provided with little pots called spittoons. It was the job of the junior nurses to empty, clean and recycle these little pots. It was a job that made me gag, and if I could get out of it I would. It was revolting and still the thought of it makes me shudder. Thank goodness times have changed and everything is disposable these days, much better for the poor student nurses.

We would do six weeks or more on a ward and then go back into school for more education. After being in the classroom for a week or more, we would be assigned to another ward. As time went on, we all got a little more confident about what we were doing.

Several girls who had started with us had now left, so our numbers were dwindling slowly. We were all looking forward to going into our next year of training as we would then not be at the very bottom of the ladder and would hopefully not have to do some of the most hated jobs as there would be new students who would take our place.

Flipping Exams

The end of year exams were dreaded by all. We were expected to do our revision in our down time, which looking back was very little. We were working at least 40hrs a week, early mornings, late evenings and nights. Looking back, I don't know how we managed it. I remember sitting an exam after 10 days of shifts just feeling exhausted, the deed was done and I had 2 days off. I was going home to my parents. I am afraid I was very unsociable and just slept. I did not think about how difficult it was as it was just part of the job.

Something else I had to learn when I went home was not to go into gory details about what I had seen, especially at the meal table. My siblings did not have such strong stomachs as I did. Mum had to point out that they were pushing their plates away when things got too much for them.

I passed my end of year exams, and I was now on the right road to becoming a nurse. Times were changing. Students could now call each other by their Christian names. Our lives were becoming a little easier. Although we still worked very hard, the hours were becoming better. Doctors seemed to mellow a bit and we were not so afraid of them, but thought of them as a member of the team.

One of the most hated shifts was starting at 7.30am working till 12mid day then off duty till 4pm and working till 9pm. It was a killer and we could be given 5 or 6 of these in a row, very little time to have a social life or find a soul mate. Thankfully, these shifts were stopped, and the hours became more manageable. It was either an early late or night shift. Most of us hated nights, but it was just a hill we had to climb. Nights started at 9pm and finished at 7.30am.

We had a meal break at about 1am and had to go to the canteen. The food was awful at night. I have not eaten plump sausages since my training. Fat sausages full of gristle are not very palatable at the best of times, but at 1 or 2 in the morning they are gross.

We often got called back to the ward if there was an emergency as there were only two nurses on at night, and the 1st or 2nd years we had left in charge were often worried about being left. I don't blame them. It's a big responsibility to be left in charge of about 34 patients who were all ill. I never minded being called back especially if sausages were on the menu.

Towards the end of my training the hours got even better. We were not allowed to work for more than 7 days without a day off. It was different with each ward, or whether you were flavour of the month. You could get 2 days off together, or split throughout the week.

Third years were the senior students and wore blue belts to signify how far they were in their training. We were expected to run the wards, do the drug rounds, and teach the 2nd and 1st year students. I remember asking one student if she would go into a side room and clean up a patient who had had an accident. I was told in no uncertain tones to do it myself. Wow, I would never have dared say that. I told her it had to be done, and I would do it with her. All patients needed to feel clean and cared for. With great huffing and puffing she came with me.

I asked this student at a later date why she wanted to be a nurse. She informed me she did not but her mum and dad had made her. Well she did not last very long, that can only be good for the profession. I heard later she had become a hairdresser probably this suited her a lot better.

Whilst I was training I had constant support from my lovely parents, and also from one of my old teachers. She was great, she used to come to the nurse's home and bring fish and chips or just encourage me to keep going. I am still in contact with her today, and in fact, she is my eldest daughter's godmother. She would take me out for lunch, or take me shopping, and was always interested in what I had been doing.

I don't know if everyone keeps in contact with their teachers, but she has always been a part of me and my family life. She would have loved to have had children of her own, but unfortunately, she had suffered two ectopic pregnancies so was unable to conceive.

Life is so unfair sometimes she would have made a great mum. Her husband was a darling who was always supportive to me and my family. He died seven years ago and obviously she was bereft, so I try to see much more of her these days.

Chapter 5
In My Third Year

During my 3rd year when we thought we were the best thing since sliced bread, I met my husband. He was a patient on the ear nose and throat ward where one of my friends was working. She went out with his visitor, and I went on a blind date with my now husband. We were together for four years until we tied the knot. We have now been married for 44 years. He was tall dark handsome and a real gentleman and still is. We have two wonderful children Charlotte and Emma. Emma blessed us with identical twins George and Edward who are 11 and gorgeous and very loving. Charlotte had beautiful little girl who is 4, she is an absolute delight. I so wish my parents had got to meet our Grandchildren. They would have loved them so much.

I enjoyed working on the genealogical ward. It was a two-floor ward with a lift that was always breaking down. There were also several side rooms. In one of these rooms, when I was a 1st year, was a lady who was quite poorly. She had had a major operation and having problems recovering; I spent a lot of time with her. One morning, when I was scheduled to look after her, I went into her room and she looked awful, pale shocked and gasping for breath. I remember fetching the sister and shortly after this the lady went into cardiac arrest; my very first time of seeing this. We managed to revive her, and she went on to make a full recovery, but it stayed with me for years. When the lady went home she bought me a bracelet and I still have it.

Another thing I recall about this ward was as a very new student nurse. I was in the lift which had broken down, with a patient who had a cardiac arrest. I was terrified and was shouting for help. The sister in charge came to the lift and was shouting instructions to me on how to resuscitate the lady. Thankfully, it worked and the lady made a good recovery. I am still to this day not very fond of lifts. I avoid them whenever I can.

We had a lady on the ward who was suffering from excessive bleeding. She was scheduled to go into theatre that morning. She had 9 children and had opted to have a coil fitted to prevent her having more pregnancies. Her husband was a bit odd and would talk very loudly over her.

The poor woman couldn't get a word in edgeways. It turned out that her husband had taken her coil out with a pair of pliers, as he liked her pregnant. He did not agree with her having the coil. He had made a real mess of her. She had needed reconstructive surgery before she could go home. I think this is the first abuse case I ever came across, and it left a lasting impression on me.

I remember the police being called and him being hauled off the ward. Unfortunately, because of what he had done she needed a hysterectomy. It defies belief what some women have to put up with. What happened to her brute of a husband I do not know, I so hope he was punished for the awful crime on this poor woman.

A big job that had to be done on the Gynae ward was vulval washing, (we called it fanny bashing). Every patient who had had surgery, which was most of them, had to have this indignity twice a day. We had a trolley on which we had cotton wool, hexedine wash, and sanitary towels. It was done as a sterile procedure. How times has changed. As bizarre as it sounds, I used to enjoy doing this round as it gave me time to talk to the patients and get to know them.

From my recollection, we did not have cleaners when I first started my career and one of the daily jobs was to do the damp dusting (known as the damn dusting) of all ledges, bed tables, and bed frames. It was just part of the job and you just got on with it. Some of the sisters were paranoid about how the beds were made. All the wheels on the beds had to be pointed forwards. The pillowslips had to face in the same direction. The hospital corners on the beds were a must. It sounds ridiculous but all the wards were the same and it was just something we had to do. Every day, each patient's linen was changed so everyone had a clean bed every day.

Chapter 6
Final Examinations

The next goal was to pass my final examinations. We had a written paper and an oral, it was daunting. Eventually, I got through and most of my friends passed; we were all made staff nurses at the same time. Then we had to decide what we wanted to do. I actually failed the exam the first time I took it; I passed the written paper but failed the oral. I had a consultant who asked me to set up for a major operation, he was asking a lot. I had never done this before, so was unable to do this as he would have liked. I was so mad at myself for failing but fortunately we could retake the oral three months later. That time, I was asked to do something which I was familiar with, so was deemed proficient to work as a nurse.

I decided to work on the gynae ward. It was a difficult transition from being a student to being in charge of the ward but, with experience came calm. It was lovely to be able to help the upcoming students to reach their goals. Life was getting easier and times were changing. The students were now calling us by our Christian names and a lot of the stuffiness had gone out of life, but we still worked very hard. The hours were still long and we had to do a week of nights every six weeks which was difficult.

The wards were much quieter at night, there were no doctor's rounds, but it was difficult to get all the work done as there were only two members of staff on duty. We didn't have auxiliary nurses to help at that point. We seemed to make endless cups of tea for patients and were on the go most of the night.

We had a drug round to do at 10pm by which time some of the patients were asleep and we would wake them up to ask them if they needed a sleeping tablet, bizarre, but that's what we did.

Patients who were going to theatre the next day had to be prepared before the day staff came on duty. The other patients all had to have their breakfast and that needed to be cleared away also before the day staff arrived. The poor patients were eating their breakfast at 6am and sometimes earlier, so that we could get finished. Most of them were fine and very thankful for the care that we gave them.

After I started going out with Richard it became more difficult to make arrangements as we never knew from one week to the rest what we were working, somehow, we managed it. It takes a special man to put up with the hours that a nurse works, thankfully it worked out for us. I remember on one occasion I had not seen him for days. I was supposed to be on an early 7.30–5.30 but had to stay on as someone had gone off sick.

I asked him to come to the ward and he agreed, so we could go out after I had been relieved. The minute he got there a colleague told me that the matron was doing her rounds, so I had to hide him in the kitchen. Thank goodness he wasn't found, I dread to think what the consequences would have been. As they say needs must.

We still had to live on the premises. This is a little difficult when you have a boyfriend. I don't think students would put up with that these days. When I was a staff nurse I was moved into a house along with several other colleagues and it became easier to bring our boyfriends in, but it was very much frowned on.

Gynae was a busy ward and run with military precision. The Sister in charge was extremely old school. She was called the Sargent major by most of the nurses. She was a really good nurse and just wanted the best for her patients. We had a morning meeting at 7.30am and beware any one turning up late. It was tough but she taught me a lot. I worked with her for a year, and then transferred to the women's surgical ward.

The surgical ward was busy with patients going to the theatre every day during the week. After operations patients were kept in bed for several days. Someone having their appendix out would be on the ward for at least seven days. I believe these days they go home the next day. I am sure this is better for their recovery. We had quite a few patients who had a blood clot in their legs after surgery. We know better now, get them up as soon as possible after surgery, and get them to wear flight socks so that does not happen.

One of the consultants who graced the ward was awful. He was rude and had the bedside manner of a goat. I remember vividly one lady who had come in for a hernia operation. He went to her bedside, pulled her nightdress up and said very loudly, "No wonder you have a hernia, you are too fat."

The whole ward heard it. I felt so sorry for her. She was only in her early twenties and was absolutely mortified. This would not be allowed these days. Thankfully, doctors seem much more human now. I suppose it was the professions fault. Consultants were treated like Gods. The way they spoke to their patients and some of the junior doctors was not even civil, it was awful.

Becoming a staff nurse was totally different to being a student. You were expected to run the wards, do the doctor's rounds, teach the students and work at the same time. It was difficult to get used to but it was what we had all worked towards so we just got on with it. In time, it became easier and we all became more confident. As staff nurses, we still had to live in and soon after this some of us were transferred into a large house near the hospital. It was a huge house with large bedrooms, but unfortunately, I had the room that had the boiler in it. It was noisy twenty-four hours a day and extremely hot. I found that I was suffering from lack of sleep and was pleased when another room became available so I could move, that was such a relief.

The girl that moved into my old room came from the Caribbean, loved the heat and also the noise didn't keep her awake, so thank goodness for that.

Richard used to come and visit me, I recall on one occasion I was reported to the hospital for having a man in my room. Oops! I wasn't the only one but looking back, it was so old fashioned and ridiculous. There was a lady living in downstairs who was there to keep an eye on us. She would let herself into our rooms at any time so we were quite restricted in what we could do. We were getting married a few months later, but that's how things were. Nowadays, there would be a revolt if these were the rules. How times change.

Chapter 7
Onto Midwifery

Two years after passing my final exams, I thought perhaps I should add to my qualifications and was talked into doing midwifery. This was a yearlong course split into 2 six-month sections, called part 1 and part 2.

For part 1, I went to Watford. Don't ask me why, but it was a new maternity hospital perhaps that's what made me go there. Midwifery was totally different to general nursing ladies were still called patients, but they were not ill and it seemed a lot friendlier environment.

Back to Being a Student

I applied to the new maternity unit called Shrodell's wing in Watford. After an interview was offered a place on the course. So, my career as a midwife began. We had to live on the premises.

The accommodation was good as it had only just been opened, but very hot. We had a room each with a row of baths and loos at the end of the corridor. I quickly got to know my student colleagues and we formed a tight group and supported one another throughout our training.

We were a smallish student group of twelve girls. We quickly made friends and would help one another to understand anything that we or them did not understand. One of the things I found difficult was the different blood groups, and the positive and negatives of these. One of the girls who was actually a nun, sat me down, explained it to me in plain English and I have never forgotten it.

It was a big thing to go back to learning from the beginning again. I found it difficult to sit for hours in a classroom, after being on the wards all the time. I found most of the learning easier as I had my nurse training behind me, but spending your evenings studying after running the wards did not come easily.

One of the things we had to do was work in the milk kitchens. In those days we had to sterilize all the bottles and teats, also make up the feeds for every baby in the hospital. We had to wear white plastic aprons, hats, rubber gloves and a face mask. It was a very hot job. The milk of choice was carnation milk, which came in the tins as it does now.

All of these had to be opened, and the milk diluted for every baby. After the feeds, the bottles would be returned to the milk kitchen then they were cleaned and brushed ready for the next feed. It was a huge task. Thank goodness it doesn't happen now. Baby's milk comes ready prepared with a sterile teat for each baby.

When we went to see our first birth we all stood round at the end of the lady's bed, all gawping in expectation, about 20 of us – how awful is that. Several students fainted, but all I can remember is the wonder of it all. Would I ever learn how to do this like these midwives who were working in the delivery ward? When you look back on this experience it is absolutely awful that we all stood round staring. It is not a spectator sport, nor the way to encourage a nice low key natural place for a woman to give birth.

As a student midwife, we had to deliver 10 babies with another midwife's hands over ours, then deliver 30 alone with mentor looking on. Delivery wards in the 70's were not like they are now. Ladies did not have a dedicated midwife. It was any one who happened to be there at the time of delivery. Students were literally running for each delivery. As a student, we went room to room checking blood pressures, babies' heart rates checking temperatures, it was very impersonal.

Midwifery records were also very different. Ladies had a card called a co-op card. *This* consisted of front page with mother's details, second and third page held her antenatal care, and back page the delivery page. When you look back on that paperwork to what midwives have to fill in now it has gone the other way. There is so much paperwork now it takes a good hour to fill it in after each delivery. Then along came the computer – now that's a different story.

Watford had underfloor heating which was great for the patients, but not for the staff. In the nursing home we couldn't stand the smell of our shoes so they were relegated to the outside window sill. This was ok until it snowed and we were putting on wet freezing cold shoes. Not good for our health but those shoes stank, I was so pleased when I could throw them away at the end of my part 1 experience.

We had to work day and night shifts whilst in training and night shifts were quite trying. The babies were all kept in the nursery at night, only the breast-fed babies were taken to their mothers for feeds. The bottle-fed babies were fed by us.

I remember one night one baby in particular was very unsettled. It was keeping all the other babies awake. So, in my wisdom I decided to separate this baby from the others. The only place I could think of to place it was in the bathroom. The baby settled down and went to sleep and we got on with our duties. Then the night-sister arrived to do a round. Of course, at that moment the baby in the bathroom started to cry, the sister was not amused. I got a dressing down and was asked how I would feel if it was my baby that had been put in the loo. I shouldn't have done this, but desperate times call for desperate measures. I did tell the lady in the morning about what had happened. She was lovely and said to me, I don't blame you he has the loudest cry on the ward. So, I didn't feel so bad after that. Women are so lovely.

The first deliveries I did were so frightening. A midwife was always in the room with you but it is so scary to think you were in charge of this delivery. I never thought I would ever feel confident enough to be on my own.

After we had done 10 deliveries with the midwives' hands over ours, they upped the ante. The midwife was still in the room; but did not interfere unless you were doing something they didn't like. I eventually felt more confident but the thought of being on my own without backup was so frightening, although help was always available at the press of a button.

With each delivery it got a little easier, but I really never felt in control at first. It's a huge responsibility delivering babies. It took me a long time to get used to the idea of being in charge, although I loved every minute of it.

Going back to being a student again after being a staff nurse is quite difficult. You were at the bottom of the ladder again, had to cope with that, as well as the mounds of paperwork and books we were expected to read.

I always envied people who could draw well. I cannot draw a straight line without a ruler. Some of my drawings of certain body parts did not look at all as they should have done. As a tutor said to me, it was not my forte. She was being kind when she said that. It was appalling, however hard I tried, it never looked right.

I eventually got through my first part of training and then came the exams, they were always daunting. I was lucky that I passed and could go on to the next stage of my training. It was sad to leave all my friends behind but most of us were departing to another hospital, so that made it easier. The bonus was I was much nearer to Richard, and my family.

Chapter 8
On to the 2nd Half of My Midwifery Training

I went to Northampton for my part 2 midwifery. No underfloor heating so that was a bonus, also not far from where my parents lived which was great, and much nearer to Richard. I enjoyed my training at Northampton but not the course work – this was never my favourite thing, but thankfully, I was so interested in the subject it made it easier so eventually I passed and became a fully qualified midwife, but it took a lot of effort.

During this last six months of training we were given a mentor midwife. Well I struck gold. Mine was an absolute darling. Hard working, extremely knowledgeable, and lovely with it. When she got to know me, she allowed me to attend patients on my own for their postnatal visits. At the time I did not drive, so had to go to these visits on the bus. We were given bus tickets by the maternity unit.

During the night, we had to call a taxi if we were attending a birth before the midwife. It was a very slow way of working. We could not fit many visits into a day. We also carried heavy bags, which contained all the equipment we needed. The top of the bag turned into a Sterilizer which we could set up at the patient's house to boil our equipment.

I remember visiting a patient with my mentor. Just before we went in she told me that it was a bit of a strange household. She was not wrong. We were invited into the house. What a tip. There was a table piled high with rotting food, the baby was on the settee cuddled up to large dog. There were also two double mattresses on the floor with several people on them. God only knows who they were. The smell was unbelievable. It was not a pleasant visit. The final straw for me was when a mouse ran over my foot. I have never shot out of a house so quickly, ugh.

Outside the house was an ice cream van that the family ran. I have never since that day had or allowed my children to have that range of ice cream!

Chickens in the House

Another visit I will always remember was to a lady who had just had her 6th child. They were all aged from 7 down, so she really had her hands full. My mentor was with me and said to me you may be surprised by this household. I was thinking to myself after what I have seen recently; I would be shocked if I was surprised by anything. Well we went in. There were dogs, chickens, and ducks in the house. The noise was unbelievable. Children shouting. Dogs barking, chickens clucking. My mentor was right I was shocked. The worst thing was the smell, and the fleas. It was thankfully our last visit of the day.

I remember getting back to the nurses' home, jumping into the bath fully dressed. How those children survived I do not know. It is very sad to see children being brought into the world to live in desperate situations. They were obviously a happy family and the children seemed well nourished, so in those days there was not a lot we could do about it. I just hoped I did not have to return to that house.

I learned to drive during my training at Northampton and it was a scary time. Neither of my parents had driven cars, although my dad had driven during the Second World War. I failed my first test, by backing into a dustbin. The examiner looked at me and I knew that was that. Fortunately, I passed at the second attempt, so I was let loose on the Nation's roads. Richard let me drive his car, but I think I frightened him to death on occasions, I certainly scared myself.

As I have written, my first home birth I attended alone was a twin birth. I thought that was scary. The very next delivery I was sent to was worse I think. The lady was having her first baby. I got to the house and when I examined the lady I found she was five centimetres dilated with a breech baby.

My mentor was on a day off so I called her relief who told me that she had seen the lady the day before and that the baby was head down. She told me it was probably a bald head.

I was not convinced, I asked the midwife if she would attend and she told me that she would come after she had finished her supper.

I was really anxious but tried to remain calm, talking the lady through her contractions and listening in to the baby's heartbeat.

The midwife had still not arrived when the lady told me she wanted to push. I rang the midwife again to be told she was on her way. All I was thinking was, I hope she hurries.

The baby's bottom appeared at the same time as the midwife. I have never been so relieved to see someone in my whole life. The midwife was still questioning the baby's position as the bottom appeared. She leapt to her feet and sprang across the room. We both encouraged the lady to push so that the rest of the baby would deliver.

Fortunately, the baby delivered quite quickly and cried straight away. I was never so relieved. I felt like I needed a drink and a lay down.

The relief midwife was very apologetic that she had not believed me. I was just grateful she had arrived when she had. It is always good to have a lot of practice doing deliveries whilst you are in training. I just thought I would like a few normal births to save my shredded nerves.

These day's student midwives are not left on their own to go to women in labour. The midwife is always with them. When they have qualified they have a year with a mentor so that they gain confidence to work alone.

Towards the end of our training, we were expected to deliver patients on our own with the midwife outside the door. Oh my goodness, that was scary. Times were changing and husbands were usually in the delivery rooms with their wives, so at least you had the husband to press the bell if you needed help.

I remember vividly the first baby I delivered on my own. They were lovely couple having their first child. The lady was doing very well but was very vocal when she had a contraction. I learnt a few new swear words that day. The husband was shocked by his wife's language, but I told him that it was fine and I had heard it all before. (some of it.)

Chapter 9
Home Births and Alone

Going out to home births on your own was always daunting, you never knew what you were going to find until you got there. Usually things worked out and my mentor midwife was always at the end of the phone if I needed her. The midwives always turned up for the delivery and watched alertly to see that we were in control of what we were doing. There were very few scans done in those days, so we sometimes got surprised by a breech birth, or a baby with a defect or even twins. Fortunately, most of the time things turned out well, and we left a happy mum and dad with their babies.

Six weeks before our final exams we had to go back into the Maternity Unit. We were expected to do deliveries on our own, only asking for help if we were unsure.

I was asked to look after a young patient who was accompanied by her mother and boyfriend. She was having her first baby. The noise coming from the room was loud. Screaming, shouting, swearing. My ears were ringing. I could not make myself heard. She was clutching her boyfriend's hand and he was shouting as she was squeezing too hard.

I tried to calm the situation down. The girl's mother was telling her to be quiet, which was not helping. It turned out that the girl had got pregnant the first time she had had sex. She was very scared and did not understand the process of birth. Her mother was telling her it was her own fault she was in pain and she had to put up with it.

This was not very helpful. I asked the mother if she would like to go and get herself a cup of tea and take the boyfriend with her. Thankfully, she agreed. I then had time to talk to the girl and find out what her worries were. Poor thing, she did not even know where the baby came out. I talked her through it and she calmed down and started to breathe through her contractions.

When her mother and boyfriend came back, they were shocked to see how in control she was. I was so proud of her. She was totally in the moment and went on to have a normal delivery some time later. She was a natural with her baby and a few days later went home to start her new life.

Many years later, I was shopping with a friend when a lady came up to me and asked me if I was a midwife. It turned out it was this same girl. That was more than twenty years later. I was shocked that she remembered me but she told me her child was now twenty-three and was a nurse. She herself had gone on to have three more children with the same boyfriend. I was so pleased for her. She told me that she had made sure her children knew all about the birds and the bees.

Final Exams

Finals were heading towards us. We had a written paper, which was three hours long, then had to go to London for a viva. It was a terrifying time for us all. We had many sleepless nights cramming into the wee small hours. I remember my oral examination vividly.

We were taken into a large room. There was a doctor and a senior midwife sitting at a table. Questions were fired at us. Then we were introduced to a pregnant lady who we had to examine abdominally, and report back.

My hands were shaking but the lady was so lovely. I examined her and thought to myself, *I think this is twins*. I looked at the lady, and said I think you are expecting twins. She whispered to me, I am having twins, and they are both breech.

I managed to locate the babies' positions and listened to their heartbeats. We had no Sonicaid then, it was done with a pinard, which looks a bit like a trumpet. I reported back to the examiners and they were suitably impressed. I saw the look of surprise on the Midwives face. I was so grateful to that lady and I passed with flying colours. That was a first. I usually just managed to get over the pass mark. I now had to look for a job. I worked in the unit I had trained in for a while then decided to branch out.

When I became a fully qualified midwife I was expected to teach students. This is a huge transition for someone who is just starting out, trying to gain your own confidence, actually we learnt from one another.

Most students were great, really interested in what was happening, and it was becoming more relaxed in the delivery wards with husbands now usually in attendance. I remember one lady who was having a difficult time coping with her contractions.

Her baby was in the posterior position, which meant its back was along her back. This can be really painful. The husband was less than sympathetic and kept saying to her I don't know what all the fuss is about. In the end I got so fed up with him putting her down, I said to him. How would it feel if you had a clamp put on your penis every 3 minutes and left it there for a minute? His face was a picture, it did the trick. He was much more supportive after that.

I gained a lot of experience working in Northampton. I worked on the delivery ward and the ante and post-natal wards and thoroughly enjoyed it, but my vision was to work in the community. I was looking to the future to enable me to do this. I also did not want to be working long shifts for the rest of my life, this was another reason I decided community was best for me.

In the first year after becoming a midwife I delivered about 40 babies, so gained quite a bit of confidence. Working in the unit was lovely, but I was getting ready to get married and wanted to get onto the community so that I would not be working shifts forever. I knew I would have to do on calls, and that seemed a good swop for a week of nights every 6 weeks. I knew it was going to be a challenge but felt I was ready for it. I was moving to another phase of my career.

I found out that a community job was coming up in the near future so with crossed fingers I put in for an interview. My old mentor midwife was very encouraging to me and told me to go for it. So, I put in my application...

Chapter 10
Becoming a Community Midwife

I went for an interview and managed to obtain a job on the community as a nurse/midwife. This meant I was going to ill patients, then maternity patients. Working on community was a lovely job, but my sense of direction was never good, and I was forever getting lost. I had passed my driving test not long before I got the job so it was a difficult transition. I was able to live at home, the only problem was my parents did not have a land line, not many people did in 1970, one was installed and off I went.

My supplied car was a heap of rust, but only failed me once. I was driving along a country road and a back wheel flew off. Scary but in my uniform a very nice man stopped, retrieved the wheel from the field put it back on for me and I continued on my way.

The first births that I did on my own after leaving the safe haven of the hospital were daunting. Alone in a house with basic equipment and lots of apprehension. There was no pressing a bell for help. I was lucky I had no problems with the first deliveries but remember well going to a lady who belonged to another midwife who was on leave.

She was quite a large lady, and I found it difficult to work out which way the baby was laying. It seemed to me that the baby was breech, but the woman insisted I was wrong. Her own midwife had told her the day before that her baby was head down. I examined the lady and found she was 9cm with a bottom of the baby presenting. This lady needed transferring to the hospital for a safe delivery, so I asked her husband to phone for an ambulance. He informed me that they did not have a phone, so I asked him to go to the phone box nearby to ring, and to be quick about it.

I was terrified but tried to remain calm. I asked the lady to breathe and not to push. Well that didn't work, she pushed anyway. The husband reappeared just as I was delivering the baby. He started running around in circles saying, "This is awful. What do we do now?"

I looked at him and said, "We deliver the baby."

The lady was pushing with her contractions until the presenting bottom appeared. The husband then said it has got an ugly face, and it's bald. Well I said that's its bottom, I am sure that the face will be more beautiful. That got him more worried, he was freaking the mother out when the ambulance arrived. Thank goodness, some back up. I told them what was happening and they both looked at me and informed me neither of them have ever delivered a baby head down let alone breech. It was up to me then.

I managed to deliver a rather large baby with a headful of hair, to which the father said, he looks like a toddler, to be quite honest he did. He weighed 10lbs. I was gob smacked, but very relieved.

Thankfully the ambulance wasn't needed, although I could have done with a lay down afterwards. It gave me quite a few sleepless nights thinking about what could have happened. It also gave me a lot of confidence. It showed me that I was able to do the job I had signed up for.

I worked in a very rural area covering all the villages and was forever getting lost. My map reading had never been good and has not improved, but I managed to find my way around most of the time, I seemed to be doing a lot of general nursing and not a lot of midwifery so was looking forward to my forth coming marriage. I had been successful when I had applied for a community midwives job in Milton Keynes which is where I would be living and was looking forward to it.

One general patient I saw on a regular basis had Multiple Sclerosis. I was so fond of her. We spent many hours chatting about life. When I married Richard in 1972 she and her husband turned up at my wedding. It was so lovely to see them, and as two people had dropped out at the last minute, we were able to ask them to the reception. This lady died very soon after this, I often think of her. She was so young and beautiful.

Chapter 11
Into Married Life and Pastures New

The day of my marriage had arrived. I and my bridesmaids were driven to my family home by Richards uncle. He was a lovely man and had a great sense of humour. We all arrived safely and duly got into our dresses. The car arrived to take us to the wedding and the ceremony went well. Then it was time for the photographs.

We were married in November and it snowed, it was freezing, but we got through the photos and off we went to the reception. The reception was lovely and went really well. Then we went to Torquey for our honeymoon. One of the things I remember, is that we bought Monopoly to play whilst we were there. Seems a strange thing to do on honeymoon but it obviously was right for us.

After our marriage we moved to New Bradwell which is now part of Milton Keynes, and I started my new job as a community midwife. We moved into the nurse's house in not a very salubrious area, but we were happy there, and I carried on with my district job.

Richard's parents lived on a farm and I remember his mum visiting and bringing us some lovely lamb chops. She went on to tell me that they came from the lambs I had fed the week before. I couldn't eat them, but had to watch Richard tuck in.

In 1975, we moved into our own house in Newport Pagnell and life carried on until I had my first daughter, Charlotte, in 1976. She was such a blessing to us. She was a very easy baby who we both doted on. A first grandchild for both of our parents, so she was very much loved.

I found it quite different being pregnant and being on the other side of midwifery. But, my pregnancy went well and I worked until I was 28wks pregnant, which is what ladies used to do. I was still doing on calls until I left for my maternity leave. That is when we moved into our house in Chicheley. At 28wks of pregnancy is not a good time to move. I was in charge of the kettle and a good friend of ours moved us in a cattle truck. What the neighbours thought I do not know.

Working on your own as a community midwife can be daunting and lonely. I got very fond of all my patients, it was lovely to follow them throughout their pregnancies, sometimes delivering them, then seeing them at home with their babies. With each delivery I gained more confidence, and gradually I became more proficient and relaxed about my work.

Shortly after I was married we were supplied with bleeps, if the bleep went off we had to find a phone and then ring the hospital. We had these bleeps for many years and they did the job at the time, but times would change and we would be provided with mobile phones.

Well, mobile phones brought many joys and many problems. The network coverage was poor in many areas, and my home in a village was one of these. The only place I had coverage when I was on call was on the top shelf of a book case which was situated above the bed. When I heard the phone go off, I would have to stand upright on the bed to answer it. This was a ridiculous thing to have to do. To be woken up and have to leap upright to answer it, my poor husband thought I had lost the plot. This went on for several years until the coverage improved.

The phones we were given were very cheap and very basic, but all of us found them to be a pain in the butt. Managers would ring and ask us to do things when we were in the middle of a clinic, or driving, and then ask us why we didn't answer our phones. As time went by we were issued with better phones, and they became very useful. All my patients had my phone number and could ring at any time. This in the most part was very helpful but could be quite time consuming but leads to better care.

Chapter 12
Becoming a Mother

Charlotte was born in 1976 after a long delivery, during which I sustained a third-degree tear. (An extended tear which goes into the anus). This broke down after a few days. It was fairly horrendous and poor Richard had to pack it for several weeks. I must admit it gave me a dread of having another baby, although I knew I wanted one the thought of going through the process again was not easy.

Giving birth as a midwife is very strange, I thought I knew it all, it turned out I knew nothing, I found the process of the contractions difficult and painful. I was shocked at how painful it was and vowed to be much more understanding when I went back to my day job.

Richard was with me throughout my delivery. He was reading a book and kept laughing. I was high on gas and air and thought that he was laughing at me. It was very bizarre. Whilst I was in the pain of labour one of the GPs I worked with came to visit me. He was in the hospital on another matter and heard that I was in delivery ward. It was very kind of him but I was not at my best.

I was delivered by the senior sister who I knew from my training. She was a lovely midwife and was very kind, as she didn't deliver many babies at that time I thought it was very kind of her to look after me.

After Charlotte she was born we decided that full time work would be difficult as Richard was often away with his job, so I obtained a job on nights at a small maternity unit in Newport Pagnell.

I earned nearly as much doing two nights as I did full time on days, so this worked very well and Richard's mum very kindly looked after Charlotte for one day a week so I could get some sleep. It's a bit different working at nights when you have a baby, you cannot just go to bed when you are tired, you have to keep going, but eventually we worked it out.

Having your own child is an eye opener as far as I am concerned, I thought I was a good midwife before I had Charlotte, I think I was a very different one after her birth. It taught me patience, and if a woman wanted pain relief or to shout I encouraged them. I sometimes wish I had had my children in today's climate of midwifery, I really feel I would be better at it, especially with the knowledge that I have now, as to what I knew then. Midwifery is much more women-centred these days.

When I gave birth; you were given an enema, (to wash out the bowel), which when you are in; pain is awful. You were told to get on the bed, lay flat on your back and a pethidine injection was given in your backside. How times change, thank goodness that does not happen anymore. Ladies are given choices and are listened to. But in those days that is what they did, and women went along with it. We knew no better in those days, thank goodness times have changed.

Chapter 13
Working in a Small Maternity Unit

When I was getting ready to go back to work after Charlotte's birth, I knew that community work would not be easy long term as Richard was often away during the week. When she was about nine months old I was offered a part time post at a small maternity unit near where we lived.

The Westbury was a great maternity unit and I learnt a lot there. There was only one midwife on duty at night with an Auxiliary nurse to help. It had 12 beds 2 delivery wards, was on 2 floors with no lift – that caused a few problems for the poor women. Sometimes you had no deliveries at night but one night I remember we had four.

I still have nightmares that those women did not get the right baby the next day, but I never heard otherwise. We had a nursery which had room for all the babies, they were taken into the nursery at night and brought out to the breast-feeding mums at feed time, the bottle-fed babies were fed by us, how life has changed now.

All the babies were fed on a four hourly basis and in between these times we just had to keep them going with cuddles. The Westbury had its own cook, and the food was excellent. I still remember her scones, they were huge and delicious and if we were lucky some were left over and we could indulge ourselves.

If women ran into problems with their birth we would call in the GP. They would arrive at any time and perform forceps deliveries and stitch patients up as well. If a woman needed a caesarean we had to call an ambulance and get them to take us up the M1 to Northampton, leaving the Auxiliary in charge. That would never happen now, it was totally unsafe but it was what we did at the time. I remember one lady I took to Northampton who decided to push her baby out on the M1. I then had to get out of the ambulance to look which side of the border we were on so she could get the appropriate birth certificate.

Once every five years, all midwives at the time had to go on a residential course for a week for updating. This was usually far from home and when Charlotte was 18 months old my time had come. I was sent to York. We had to be there on a Sunday evening and stay until 5pm on Friday. I had never left Charlotte before for such a long time and it was really difficult, but my parents had her for a week and took her to the seaside in a caravan. She had a lovely time but I found it extremely difficult to be away from her for so long.

The week consisted of lecture after lecture. Our days were long, and sometimes a trifle boring. It was lovely not having to cook for a week, but I was so pleased when Richard arrived on the Friday to pick me up. Thankfully these days this does not happen. Midwives are updated in the hospitals in which they work and this is far better for everyone.

Pregnant Again

In early 1978 when Charlotte was twenty months old, I became pregnant with my 2nd child but continued to work my night shifts. One night, I remember we had bats flying about in the unit which absolutely terrified me. We had no one to call, so in desperation I called the police and they offered to send Bat Man. The police did come, they opened all the doors and tried to convince me the bats were gone, I still think they were just telling that to calm me down as they didn't want the midwife in charge going into labour.

The Sister in charge of the unit sometimes popped in at night to do a spot check, she also brought her husband with her who went around talking to the women. This was at 2 or 3 in the morning so was not very well received.

When the unit got busier we had another midwife to work with us. One that I worked with was Spanish. A nice gentle woman, but very reluctant to deliver babies, which I found very odd, but as I loved deliveries I just got on with it.

One night, we had just gone on duty when the manager arrived, she asked me to start the evening work and after a short time, she came and told me that I was on my own for the night. It became known the midwife I was working with had been struck off the midwife's register, so was working illegally, which we found quite shocking. We were back to being the lone midwife for a while.

Midwives who have been struck off these days would not be able to find work again, as each hospital checks the status of their midwives before they are employed with the Nursing and Midwifery Council.

My daughter Emma was born in November of 1978; another beautiful little girl with red hair like her mother. I had had a difficult pregnancy with Emma and was admitted to hospital 6 weeks before her birth with pre-eclampsia. (High blood pressure). Children were not allowed to visit, so I didn't see Charlotte for all that time and again Richard's mother came up trumps and helped Richard with her care.

I had an emergency section with Emma as she decided to come into the world upside down. The night before she was born unbeknown to me Richard was in a car accident. On the day of her delivery, I was quite upset when he didn't arrive at the time he had been told to be there. Shortly after this, his parents arrived and said Richard was doing some special shopping, which I thought a bit odd, but took it as true. A while after this the Salvation Army officer arrived. (My parents were salvationists), which I thought was very odd.

A few minutes later, the sister on the ward bristled in came over to me and said nothing to worry about. "Your husband has had a little bump." Then Richard arrived, dried blood all over his face walking with a stick; and trousers cut up to his knees. I remember crying hysterically, and the Army Officer started praying. Bizarre or what.

When I was taken to theatre, Richard was placed in my bed; a first for the maternity unit and probably a last. Fathers were not allowed in theatre and I was under general anaesthetic so was out for the count. When I came around, I thought that it had all been a bad dream, but obviously it wasn't.

I was in hospital for a week and asked Richard to bring in a going home outfit. That was a big mistake; I left Northampton wearing a black skirt that was tight and short, also a white blouse that was bursting at the seams. I looked like a lady of the night and have never forgotten it.

Having two children is a different kettle of fish, life was much busier. Charlotte was nearly three and was starting play school. Richard was still working away from home; sometimes I felt like a single mother. Getting out in the morning with two children is much more difficult than with one. Living in a small village means that you have to get into the car to go anywhere. How mothers cope with four or five children I don't know; I think they deserve a medal.

Richard was still working away most weeks and having a small baby and a nearly three-year-old was difficult, but eventually it got easier, and life got back to semi normal. I remember one time Richard was away and the weather was dreadful. It just snowed and carried on snowing, I was completely snowed in. Richard's father came with a tractor and dug me out, which was very helpful. Richard was also stranded where he was but I think he got the better end of the deal, he was in a hotel.

I went back on nights when Emma was 4 months old and continued at the maternity unit until the girls were both at school. The Westbury maternity unit was closing as it was not thought appropriate at this time to have small units like ours was. Now midwifery led units are popping up again. It all goes around in circles.

Going back to work after Emma was more difficult as I now had a toddler as well, but we got through it and come out the other side. I continued to work very part time with help again from Richard's lovely mum. My parents were 17 miles away and didn't drive so it was more difficult for them to help, but they supported me as much as they could.

Chapter 14
Westbury Maternity Home Is Closing

Milton Keynes hospital was opening, and the Westbury was closing. I was offered an interview for the post of community midwife. The hospital was new and I had a job finding it. Milton Keynes has an awful lot of roundabouts, but eventually I did and after the interview was offered a job.

Another type of uniform beckoned. Blue dress, blue tweed coat and pillbox hat, which never looked good on me, and the same black shoes and black tights; but no seam this time. My sense of direction was still not good and I got lost time and time again. It was before mobile phones were around and we all had bleeps which were forever going off. We had to find a phone box to ring the hospital to find out what we were needed for. Milton Keynes was not built when I first started on community.

There were about ten community midwives, all a lot older than me, and mostly single, but we were a good team. Looking back, it took me a long time to understand that the two elderly midwives, who lived together and always went on call together, had a bit of a problem with the bottle. They always drove each other about and one was particularly unsteady on her feet at times, but no one said a word. I cannot imagine that happening these days, what the patients thought I do not know.

We did not go into the hospital daily. We waited at home for the phone to ring and for visits to be given to us. We were attached to GP practices and attended ante natal clinics at these surgeries. Doctors were demi gods back then and midwives were there to be their right-hand person.

We tested the lady's urine, took her blood pressure, and sent the patients into the doctor. He would lay his hands on the lady and listened to the baby's heartbeat. Thankfully, this soon stopped and midwives took over the care of pregnant ladies with GPS being in the background, giving their support and expertise when necessary.

I was feeling quite disenchanted with the midwifery profession before we took over the main roll of looking after the women. I felt that our skills were being compromised by not being able to look after the women as we wished to. I was wondering if I was in the wrong profession. I wrote a poem, not a great poem but when I look back on that period I must have been really fed up with being a handmaiden to the doctors. Below is a copy of this poem.

You would like to be a midwife
We have a lovely life.
We are out in all foul weathers
Dragged out of bed at night.
We see patients at the clinic
We weigh and test their wee
Then send them up the corridor
To see their own GP.
They are invited to mother craft classes
The Health Visitor sees to these
Midwives make a guest appearance
They always aim to please.
When women have had their babies
And gone back home to mum
We come and poke their tum and boobs,
And peek down at their bum
Breast feeding can cause problems
We always try to help
But some mums call the NCT (National Childbirth Trust)
They think they'll sort them out.
Are midwives really needed
With the doctors and the NCT
The Health Visitors and the Government
We will stay at home and drink tea.
But NO that's not the answer
Be assertive we are told
Stand up and fight for your every right

Don't sit back and grow old.

Oh dear, not a great poet, but just shows you how things have changed, thank goodness. Midwives are now seen as practitioners in their own right. They look after the women throughout their pregnancies with input from the GPs when necessary.

I was by far the youngest community midwife and felt fully supported by my colleagues. I got very fond of some of them. Most of them were older and single. To have a young midwife who had children was very different for them. We worked well as a team, but I used to chuckle when I attended the monthly community meeting. We had one or two midwives who used to sit with their pill boxes on their heads, and their legs agape, it was not a pretty sight, but they were all excellent midwives who were very professional and kind to their ladies. I learnt a lot from them.

One of the older midwives was a really lovely lady, very rotund, who loved my girls, and was very good to them. The girls loved her and were very excited when she came to see them or I took them to see her. I worked with her for 10 years until she retired and moved away to live with her elderly sister.

Chapter 15
GP Surgeries

I worked at several different surgeries in Milton Keynes and found some of them easier than others. The friendliness at the surgery was paramount to enjoying your job. Some of the practice managers were really difficult to work with, others were human and supportive. Eventually I found my niche at a practice in Olney, a beautiful village on the outskirts of Milton Keynes.

The practice at the time was in a house on the high street. It consisted of a doctors' room, a small reception, and a very small toilet. There were two GPs working from here, one quite elderly and one young and enthusiastic. The elder of the two did not like having a midwife encroaching on his patients. Sometimes, I did not meet his ladies until they had delivered. The younger doctor and I worked together for a long time, in fact until I retired. He is still working there. He was a superb GP, extremely loved by his patients. The third GP worked out of a surgery attached to his home. He was great and we had an excellent working relationship, although sometimes I felt I needed to bring him up to the twenty first century.

One of his little ways really made me quite uncomfortable. He had a pair of marigold gloves which he used for vaginal examinations. He used to put them on then wash his hands with them on under the tap, examine the patient then he would drape them over the sink.

I took a packet of disposable gloves into his surgery but he never used them. This GP was much loved in the community and was an excellent GP. He had terrible arthritis. I remember being at a lady's house when he visited. The stairs were really steep, and he stood at the bottom and asked me to throw him a rope to help him up. He was such a lovely man. I became very fond of him. He had a wonderful sense of humour.

On one occasion a lady phoned whilst I was in the surgery with him and she was saying she needed to push, so we both decided to make our way to the lady's house which was very near to where we were. When we arrived, the woman was sitting on the toilet pushing and as we arrived she pushed her baby out into the loo. "Well done," said the doctor, "we should call him Lewie."

Milton Keynes was growing fast, and more community midwives were joining the team. As Olney was a fairly small practice at the time, I helped out at Newport Pagnell Health Centre. At that time, the surgery was on Station Road. There were 4 GPs at the time, one older; the rest up and coming doctors, young and very efficient. One of the GP was an absolute hoot. I remember the first time I met him at his clinic. I had taken the blood pressure and tested the lady's urine and was chatting to her when he came into the waiting room and said to the lady, "Get in there get um off and I will come and have a grovel."

I was very shocked but as I got to know him, I came to know that he knew which patients to say it to. They loved his banter and him. I kept Newport Pagnell going for quite a number of years, until Olney got too big to do both.

A new midwife was appointed and I remember her first day very well. A very efficient midwife. Maybe a bit low on people skills. I introduced her to a waiting room full of ladies and she introduced herself to them and told them, I am your new midwife and I hate babies.

That went down a storm, but in her favour, she was an excellent midwife; giving the best care to all her ladies. Later on, in the day after the afternoon clinic I told her you go home and I would clear up. I knew she had a young baby, who she had in a nursery. I thought she must have been longing to see her child. She informed me, its fine she has been in full time nursery since she was six weeks old. Oh well, everyone is different I suppose.

Chapter 16
Home Births

Our home birth rate was going up as the city grew. I remember many a night being pulled from by bed in the middle of the night to go to a home birth. One particular night it was extremely foggy and I had to go to Deanshanger, a village on the outskirts of Milton Keynes. A long drive in fog and I remember reaching half way I was terrified as I could hardly see where I was going. I called into a small police station and blabbed that I was on my way to a home birth but couldn't find my way.

They were extremely understanding. I was driven in a police car – the only time I have ever been in one. How they knew where they were going I do not know, I just closed my eyes and hoped for the best.

Eventually, we arrived at the house, and I was escorted up the stairs with 2 policemen in tow. They stayed for the delivery so they could escort me back to my car safely. They were extremely kind and I shall never forget their help that night. The woman and her husband were gob smacked having their baby delivered by a midwife and 2 policemen. We had a laugh about it in the days to come when I assured her I wasn't a wanted criminal but a coward in the fog.

I attended a home birth for a couple who lived in the city. I was first midwife on call so off I went. They were having their first baby and wanted everything to be as natural as possible. It was a long night of waiting for baby to come and during the conversations we were having I noticed in every room they had a picture of a very distinguished looking man and I asked who he was. That was a mistake. They told me that he was the leader of their religious group. They believed that we have all been here before.

The husband went on to explain to me that he believed he had been a woman in a previous life, and although he had given birth to children he had never had the opportunity to give birth at home so that's why they had wanted a home birth!

I quickly changed the subject. Fortunately, it was time to call the 2nd midwife, as his wife felt the urge to push. The midwife arrived and the women went on to have a lovely birth of a baby boy.

Unfortunately, we could not deliver the placenta. We tried all the usual tricks but nothing would help. We explained to the couple that we would have to transfer into the hospital as we couldn't leave her at home for much longer. The couple were very reluctant to do this and the husband said how about trying baby on the breast again as a last resort. We agreed, and although we gave them time the afterbirth was not showing any sign of putting in an appearance.

The conversation got around to calling an ambulance when the husband suddenly asked. Would it help if he sucked on the nipple! That was a first. We agreed to go into the kitchen for a few minutes to give them privacy, giving them instructions that they should watch for pain and bleeding and call us if they were worried.

After a short time – and after we had stopped laughing, I called up the stairs any luck. The father replied it is in the bucket. Well it worked and the couple got their wish of staying at home.

Another birth I attended; I was the only midwife on call, the woman was refusing to go into the hospital, so I rang our maternity care assistant Gill and asked if she would like to attend – she jumped at the chance and I picked her up and off we went.

When we arrived at the house, we took all our equipment in and introduced ourselves to a very full room. There was the girl and her partner, her father her brothers and her sister. The girl was in the birthing pool and doing very well. They were all extremely obese; and seemed constantly to be eating. Pork pies, hot dogs, crisps. They kept asking us if we wanted a pork pie, not my favourite food at the best of times and especially not in the middle of the night.

We tried to suppress our laughter but I had to send the Gill to the car at one point to get an imaginary piece of equipment as

I could see she was consumed by trying not to laugh. The lady eventually delivered and we laughed all the way home.

Later on, that year on Christmas Eve, I was on call and about 11pm I got a call for a home birth. It was a cold icy night and the roads were really slippery. After a scary trip, I arrived at the house but found it difficult to park because of the time of year. I had to leave the car a good way from the house. I took some of the equipment, and when I arrived asked the husband if he would mind coming and helping me with the rest. "Yes, I would," he told me, "it's bloody cold out there." So, off I trotted and dragged the rest of the equipment into the house saying "bah humbug" to myself all the way.

The woman was in full blown labour in a very small room with a double mattress on the floor. It was a quite difficult situation as I could not get at her to examine her, and she was reluctant to move, but we managed and I called the 2nd midwife who arrived soon afterwards. The baby was duly delivered to the sound of recorded Jeremy Kyle on the television – that was a joy.

We spent some time clearing up making sure mum and baby were well. We made to leave, asking the husband if there was any chance of some help with the equipment. This time the baby was his excuse, so we struggled on the icy paths on our own. Not a very Christian start to the holiday period but as I had been up for 8 hours I got to spend Christmas day with my family so that was good.

Funny Situations

I visited a family in a village in Milton Keynes for a colleague who was on a day off. I knew that the family were Indian and spoke very little English.

I was admitted into the house, and led into the lounge, where I found quite a few women. There was a lady sitting on the sofa holding a baby so I presumed she was the patient.

I was talking to the ladies and they were all nodding and smiling. I asked if I could have a look at the baby and I was handed a little boy with a head full of thick black hair. I examined him and he was fine. I then asked if I could feel the lady's tummy and look at her stitch line. A lady lay down and I thought to myself her uterus had gone down very well. She then turned on her side so I could take a peek at her stitches.

I was looking at her perineum thinking, I can't see anything. At that point the lady got off the settee and another lady lay down. I immediately knew I had examined the wrong patient. I was a trifle disconcerted but the ladies were all smiling and thanking me for visiting them. Well, I think that is what they were saying.

I told my colleague who knew the lady the next day and she thought it was hilarious. She told me that they all lived together and always nodded and smiled at everything. I was the butt of the joke in the community office for a good while, not surprisingly. I took it in good faith; but hoped it would not happen to me again.

I visited another family who did not speak English but I had been told that when I got to the house the mother would ring her husband who worked at a restaurant in the next street.

I arrived at the house and the mother immediately rang her husband. I was taken into the lounge. I noticed that the lady looked quite pale and very tired. The lady had four other children, who were very young, with her.

The husband arrived and I asked the usual questions. I then said to the husband that his wife looked very tired and was she getting any sleep. He told me that he was sleeping very well. I asked him to ask his wife if she was getting any sleep. He spoke to her then stated that she had been up with all the other children who had been vomiting throughout the night.

I was gob smacked, I told him that she obviously needed some help and asked if they had any relatives that could come and help. He replied that they had but they could not stay as he needed the spare bedroom so he could sleep. Unbelievable, it is very difficult to help in this situation. The language barrier meant I could not get her side of the story. It leaves you feeling a bit helpless. I did have a talk to the health visitors and they assured me that they would keep an eye on the family and would take an interpreter with them so they could get a true account of what was happening.

Young Patients

I have looked after many young patients but at one point I had two 14-year-olds. This was really unusual. They were both very different. Both lived with their parents, one was very naïve, the other seemed quite world wise. Both families were very supportive; but had different ideals. They both lived in a village, neither knew each other. One family wanted the baby to be adopted. This was the ideal solution for the girl who was so lovely. I got really fond of her and she coped with the pregnancy very well.

Fortunately, she had a normal pregnancy and coped with the delivery extremely well. She did not see her baby and this was what she wanted. I saw her several times after she delivered, she had grown up a lot during the experience. She told me that she looked forward to when her child reached eighteen and could contact her if it wanted to.

I was fortunate enough to deliver this girl's next baby when she was in her twenties and married. She was not living in my area but I agreed to look after her. She had a home delivery and talked about the baby she had had adopted with affection. She had a really lovely birth and I was so thrilled for them both.

The other young girl was more difficult to look after. Her parents would not let her come to the surgery as they did not want the neighbours to know what was happening. I agreed to visit her at home and was asked to go after dark and not wearing uniform.

During the light evenings this became quite difficult. The parents kept her away from school and the girl was obviously upset by being kept in like this. The tension in the home was quite palpable. I felt quite sorry for the girl. I asked the mother on several occasions if I could speak to the girl alone. This did not happen. It was quite difficult to support the girl as her mother was always talking for her.

Eventually, the baby was born and the girl's parents decided to bring it up as their own. The girl did not think that this is what should happen but, obviously, she did not have the final decision. I managed to see her when she was in the hospital. She told me she thought her parents were keeping the baby to punish her for getting in the situation. I am sure this was not the reason but I hope they managed to sort things out so they could live harmoniously.

I did a visit on a young patient for a colleague who was on leave. I knew that the girl was 15 years old and had just delivered her baby. I was led into the house by a lady wearing her dressing gown. I presumed she was the girl's mother. The girl sat on the sofa cuddling the baby and asked me if I would like to see her sister. I must admit I was a bit confused and turned to the older lady. She tried to convince me that it was her baby, and she sat herself gingerly on the sofa as if she was having pain from her stitches.

I learned later that the mother had worn a cushion under her clothes so as to convince the neighbour's that she was pregnant. It was a little difficult to tell the girl's mother that I understood the young girl was the mother and I was here to make sure she and her baby were well.

The girl started crying and was obviously finding it all difficult to deal with. I told them that I was there to help and not to judge. The mother then asked me to look at her daughter but not to tell anyone that it was her baby. This was obviously my time to assure them that what happened in the house would never be discussed by me to anyone.

The girl and the baby were both well and I hope I left a happier family behind when I eventually left the house.

A Mr Whippy Job

A recent home birth took the biscuit. I agreed to cover the on call for a colleague who had an evening out booked, so up until midnight it was me. I got called about 10pm and off I trotted to the house.

When I arrived, I was shown into the lounge where a lady was kneeling on the floor against a sofa. The smell in the room was awful (Aude de toilet.) The lady told me she had had an upset tummy all day – it smelt like she still had one. Professional to the last I checked her over and found she was 8 centimetres dilated, so I called the 2nd midwife. I then asked the husband to open all the doors and windows. He didn't need asking twice – good job it was a nice evening and not freezing cold.

The second midwife arrived wrinkling her nose. This is good I whispered, you should have been here earlier. We proceeded with the delivery. All of a sudden, we heard voices talking in an Indian language and looked at one another and shrugged our shoulders. We thought the husband had put the television on. All during this time the lady stayed in the same position, and as time went on she had the urge to push so windows and doors were closed.

We encouraged the woman to do what her body was telling her to do. Unfortunately, this was not push a baby out it was to keep pooing – what I call a Mister whippy job. It was fairly horrendous, but after lots of pooh and clearing up, a beautiful baby was born to a round of clapping. We both turned around at the same time.

On the huge television were a crowd of Indian relatives who had been watching from their homeland. We waved and carried on with what we were doing but we had a good laugh in the office the next day recalling our evening out. We wondered what the onlookers must have thought at all the mess.

One night I was first on call and got a phone call about 11pm informing me that a patient had gone into labour in a nearby town. I made my way to her house and she was indeed having contractions but was in the early stages of labour.

Whilst I was at her house I got a phone call telling me one of my own ladies had gone into labour and wanted to push, so I asked the delivery ward to ring the second midwife, telling them I would make my way to Olney to see the lady who appeared to be in established labour. They agreed to do this, and I drove to Olney, by this time it was just after midnight. I arrived to find my lady was having strong contractions, she was 8cm dilated. I was relieved I had made the decision to leave the first lady and come to this lady.

I rang the delivery suite and asked them to ring the midwife who was 2nd on call and ask her to meet me at Olney. The lady progressed quickly and she was quickly fully dilated, so it was not long before she was pushing. At that point the delivery suite coordinator rang me to inform me that they could not get any response from the 2nd midwife, also that the first lady I had visited was becoming distressed and needed a midwife. Well, I obviously cannot be in two places at once, so I asked the them to ask the first lady to make her way into the hospital as my lady was about to deliver and I obviously would be tied up for the next few hours.

My lady delivered and all was well, so once she was in her bed cuddling her healthy baby, I rang the delivery suite, informing them that I was now heading back to the hospital. I was informed that the first lady was now in the maternity unit and thankfully was doing very well, and not too cross that she had been asked to transfer into hospital.

I made my way into the hospital by this time it was now 5am.I asked after the lady that had transferred in and was told she was just about to deliver, so I made my way to her room and held her hand whilst she gave birth to her beautiful little boy. I was extremely apologetic about what had happened. Fortunately, they were very accepting and told me it was fine, you were obviously needed more by the other lady. Phew, that was a relief.

I still did not know why the 2nd midwife could not be raised. I heard later that she just did not hear her phone. Thankfully, all turned out well, but after this incident all community midwives were asked to make sure they could be roused when they were needed. We all know some mobile phones have better reception in certain places than others, so all the midwives gave their landline numbers so that this situation would not happen again.

Chapter 17
Independent Midwives

On one of my nights on call I was rung by the Delivery suite, coordinator to ask if I could go in to help as they were extremely busy. Also, one of the midwives who worked on her own as an Independent midwife, so was not employed by the hospital was at a home birth for a lady who was expecting twins. They thought that from the conversations they had had with this midwife that she would have to transfer the lady in to the hospital.

I made my way into the hospital and when I got there the coordinator was on the phone. I heard her say, call an ambulance and make your way into the hospital. She looked up and asked me to get a room ready as the twin lady was on her way in. She had delivered the first baby. The second one was breech and stuck. Not a good position to be in. I went ahead and got the room ready. I also informed the special care baby unit what was happening so that they were aware and could attend to help look after the baby that had still not been delivered.

The lady arrived with the midwife who was at the birth. The first baby was well, but small and having a job to maintain its temperature. The baby was being looked at by the Paediatrician. The lady was in a supine position on the bed. On examination it was obvious that the 2nd baby was in distress; the baby was out up to its head and was not a healthy colour.

The doctor was in the room and he managed to deliver the baby by putting forceps onto the baby's head. The baby failed to breathe but with the help of the special care nurses we managed to get a heartbeat, although the baby needed to be intubated. The baby was admitted into the special care baby unit.

The lady was admitted to a postnatal ward and did very well. The first twin was also doing very well and had been transferred back to the postnatal ward so that it could be with the mother.

The next day I was in the baby unit visiting one of my ladies who had delivered her baby early. I heard that the second twin had unfortunately died, which was extremely sad. The staff on the ward were really upset about what had happened. They were very shocked by the lady's reaction to the baby's demise.

According to the staff, she had come into the unit when she was advised that her baby was not doing well. She arrived on the unit just as the baby died, and her comment apparently was, oh well, never mind I still have the other baby. How shocking, not a reaction I have seen before or wish to hear about.

The midwife concerned I am afraid had taken a lot of risks with letting this lady deliver at home. She had to answer the hospital's questions about this. Midwives who choose to work in this way do not have the backup that community midwives have, also they cannot get insurance.

I do feel sad that midwives can take such risks with babies and women's lives. I knew other independent midwives who did not appear to take such risks. They worked with the hospital to make sure they gave the best care. This lady was lucky she had one healthy baby, but it is devastating to think about what happened to the other baby. The woman herself could have lost both babies. The midwife involved with the case is not practicing any longer. She was reported to the Nursing and Midwifery Council, who looked at the circumstances.

The case went on to a hearing and unfortunately the midwife was struck off. I do wonder if she had worked within the confines of a maternity unit she would be still working. It is such a waste of a midwife.

Chapter 18
Free Birthing

Free birthing, oh what can I say. Everyone has the right to deliver their child as they wish, but I find it a bit overwhelming that some women take such risks as to birth on their own with no professional help. One weekend I was working, our manager rang to tell us that one of our women who was intending to free birth had put it on face book that she had delivered, so we needed to visit her. Guess who was elected to go!

I arrived at the house and decided not to take the scales in, but, to find out first if they allowed me to enter or to see the baby. The woman answered the door and asked how I knew she had delivered. I told her it was all over Facebook, and I wanted and needed to know that both she and the baby were well.

She reluctantly let me in but then left me standing for nearly 15mins before she reappeared on her own with no baby in tow. I asked her about the delivery and how it went; the answer was fine. Did you deliver the afterbirth? Yes, was the answer. At that moment, the husband appeared and I introduced myself and explained why I was there.

All we want from you is the paperwork for the birth certificate he told me. I explained to them I could not give them any paperwork until I knew all the details of the birth and have had a chance to examine the baby. They reluctantly let me see the baby. I asked would they like me to weigh their child, the dad agreed the mum did not. Let me go and get the scales I said maybe you can make up your minds by then. I fetched the scales and dad agreed for me to weigh the baby. This gave me a chance to see the baby stripped and to make sure that all was well with him. The baby looked well; his cord had been tied with a shoe lace so I talked to them about cord shrinking and having to replace the tie. They both sighed and told me that they had done this before, and they did not want any advice.

Just give us the relevant paperwork and we will be happy. I explained that I would leave them with notes for mum and baby but the official paperwork would come on the next visit which would be when the baby was due for a blood test. They declined the baby being checked by a doctor, and the Vitamin K that is advisable for babies to have after delivery. This is their choice but as midwives we have a responsibility to mum and baby to make sure all is well. This kind of situation can be very stressful for all the midwives and managers. Ultimately all we want is for mum and baby to be well. Sometimes you have to walk away and put it down to experience.

Some people take risks others are so desperate for a child. I had a lovely lady who had two healthy boys who longed for another child. She managed to get pregnant and unfortunately the baby had an abnormality that was incompatible with life so she lost that baby. Another two miscarriages followed this and the last one was just before I retired. I would have done anything to give that lady a baby. She is a fabulous mum and I so wanted her to succeed. Some women take risks which I find frustrating; others would do anything for a healthy baby.

One of my home deliveries was done aboard a narrow boat. It was a windy night and the swaying of the boat was difficult to cope with. I felt very nauseous. The lady was having good contractions and I sent for the 2nd midwife just before she started to push. The delivery went well and she delivered quite quickly thank goodness.

Once the placenta had been delivered and I had checked it, the husband asked if they could keep it. It is usually taken back to the hospital but I told him it was his as long as they were careful where they discarded it.

The husband went off with it and we carried on with our work. Shortly after this the husband re-entered the room with a large frying pan, in which was the cooked placenta. The smell was quite strong, which did not help my nausea. The couple asked us if we would join them in celebrating the birth by partaking in the placenta. We declined and told them we were vegetarians, which was a white lie, but we wished them happy eating and left to go back to the hospital. Some people eat the placenta some have it made into pills to stop postnatal depression, if it works for them I have no problem with it, but please don't ask me to join you.

Children and Videos

My children were getting older and were used to mum disappearing at weird times of the day and night. Thankfully, I have a very supportive husband who was very long suffering and helped out with the children whenever he could.

When we started doing ante natal classes I remember reviewing some videos of births at home to show the mums. I was in the kitchen one day and I could hear giggling coming from the lounge. I went in and my girls were watching a birth video. When the baby was born they rewound it so the baby went back into the mum; they were finding it extremely entertaining. That was the point I had to sit down and talk to them about the birds and the bees. Emma said so if the baby comes out and it's ugly you can put it back. I didn't quite know how to answer that one. She also wanted to take the video to school for show and tell – that never happened.

Chapter 19
Managers

We had many managers; some good some well less so. When the hospital first opened we had one manager, who was efficient, but as the hospital grew she was stretched fairy thin, so another manager was engaged. We went from the sublime to the ridiculous. She was a lovely lady but lacking in managerial skills. She didn't have a clue of what we did; had never been a community midwife and thought we all spent our time driving around and drinking tea. This manager didn't last very long but went off to do a health visiting course. She was better with patients than staff, and as far as I know she is still working in this field.

The next manager had a middle name of Hitler, this sounds unkind but she was really not good with staff; many a time I found colleagues in tears. I remember going into work one day and finding a colleague in tears. When we sat her down and asked her if we could help, she told us that her stepson had been found dead in their family home in the Caribbean. He was 18. This lovely midwife had looked after this child since he had been a toddler. We asked her why she was at work. We were told that the manager had told her that as it was not a blood relative she could not take any time off. Unbelievable!!! We went to the senior manager who straight away told her to go home and take the time off she needed.

This same manager made us go into the hospital each morning so she knew we were all on duty on time. Just after she started my mother was taken very ill and was admitted to hospital. I phoned in to tell my colleagues and I got a lot of support from them, the manager was a different kettle of fish.

Mum had been diagnosed with Leukaemia and was not expected to live very long, so I stayed with her. Unbeknown to me, my manager had phoned the ward, telling the staff to tell me that she expected me back on duty the next day. I was not told this until the evening, but by then, my poor mum had died.

I was extremely upset as you can imagine, I think it's the only time ever I did not obey a manager's orders. I did not return to work the next day; but phoned the senior manager, who told me to take all the time I needed. What a difference to the other manager. I am afraid I reacted very badly to her unkindness. When I returned to work and went into a meeting for community midwives I felt really ill and had to leave. I saw her and had what I know now is a panic attack, my first and thankfully my last.

I went to see my GP as I was worried about how I had reacted. He was extremely understanding. He told me what had made me react like that. His kindness and the coping skills he gave me held me in good stead for my future.

I had a phone call from that manager some weeks later. She was very tearful because her dog had died. I didn't give her much sympathy which was probably unkind, but I found it very difficult after what she had done to me.

Thankfully, her reign as manager did not continue and she was demoted to being a community midwife. All the community midwives found that was difficult to handle for a while. Thankfully, she retired early and a huge sigh of relief went around our community office.

When a parent dies I don't know if everyone feels the same but I felt very protective of my dear father spending as much time with him as I could. He coped very well and looked after himself; cooking his own meals and cleaning the house; also visiting the old folk who were actually younger than him. If I couldn't get hold of him, I would drive to Northampton where I would usually find that he was fine and had probably been in the garden when I rang.

My children were devastated by their lovely nannie's death; but coped with it all very well and supported me as much as they could. I went back to work after the funeral but found it very difficult to cope as all the babies I saw seemed to have been born on the day mum had died. I found myself in tears frequently. Life did eventually get back to some sort of normality and the work went on, sleepless nights and all.

As my children were growing up, it got easier to leave them without feeling guilty about neglecting them. I hope they never felt that. I think they just thought it was a normal way of life. They were always fishing for information about their friend's mums; Did I know so and so was pregnant and if so why had I not told them. They came to understand that, I knew about most pregnancies they were talking about but could not divulge to them until the news was out. Even now I get, "You didn't tell me so and so was pregnant, even when they are best friends." Really, they know I would not tell them, it is not my news.

Chapter 20
More Home Births

The phone rang and another home birth was on the cards; off I went and in time called the 2nd midwife; a good friend of mine and an absolute darling with the patients. We duly delivered the baby but we could not deliver the placenta so after trying all the usual tricks we called an ambulance and off we went in the ambulance, me with the lady and my colleague following in her car. We duly arrived at the hospital and delivered the lady to the midwives in the delivery ward.

Just before we left to drive back to the house to pick up my car, we remembered we had left the drug box in the house. The husband told us that he had a spare key so we could go in, get the box and put the key through the letter box. Off we went.

We arrived back at the house – it was 4am by this time and pitch black we found we couldn't fit the key in the door. After a few minutes the door opened and we were greeted by a man who asked us what we thought we were doing. We were at the neighbour's house. Fortunately, he had seen me earlier in the evening so knew we were not burglars! We quickly scarpered to the right house and picked up the drug box. We had a good laugh then and later about our little mishap.

Milton Keynes Is Growing

As time went on, Milton Keynes grew and more and more houses were built. It seems that for every new housing estate that was built, we obtained another manager. Things changed time and time again. New general practices were opened and we were busier than ever.

It got more difficult to find your way around as many of these estates did not have road names on them; also the house numbers were never where you thought they should be. Fortunately, by this time, we all had mobile phones, so could ring the patient and ask them to try to hone us in to where they were. Thank goodness for my husband buying me a sat nav. This wasn't as helpful as I thought it would be as Milton Keynes was growing at a monumental rate, and all these new streets were not on my lovely sat nav.

We managed to get to most places in time but it caused a lot of grief and patience; not to panic and think we would not get where we needed to be. It usually worked out in the end. It always surprised me when I phoned the lady to guide me to her and they did not know how to do this, frustrating but true.

As I grew older, the nights on call became more trying, I groaned when I was called but usually once on the move it was fine, but it took longer to get over a night on the tiles. The time was coming when I needed to think about cutting down my hours, the heart was willing but the body was not quite as willing. I decided to go part time. I cut down to 4 days a week.

I might have cut down on my hours but was still doing a lot of home births, in fact, I won an award for doing the most home births; pity they did not spell my name right on the plaque, but the thought was there. I still had the same number of women to look after so worked even harder to make sure everyone was happy, that they had all the help they needed.

We were a good team of midwives and everyone supported each other but it became a running joke that no one wanted to be on call with me. I seemed to be out every time I was on call. I used to think they were trying to kill the oldies off first. Actually, getting up and out of bed and working as you get older actually keeps you young, although it takes you longer to spring back to normal after a night up, it is very rewarding and knew if I stopped working I would miss it terribly.

I was very lucky to work in a superb GP practice where all staff worked well together. They were all great and extremely supportive. We made a great team. The GPs always took all of us out for a Christmas meal and we never had to pay for tea and coffee, which in most surgeries you do.

The GPs were very supportive and really nice people. I feel so lucky to have worked in such a surgery. We also had an extremely efficient and lovely Practice Manager, who I found always helpful. Some managers at the practices I had been in before were rude and unhelpful.

When rules were changed as in 'NICE' guidelines, we saw our pregnant ladies less throughout their pregnancies. I found it quite difficult to cope with. I had seen many problems happen in pregnancies and was terrified that things would get missed, so I gave my patients the option to see me more often and most of them took me up on it.

My clinics were always full but I was happy if the ladies were happy. According to Nice guidelines we had to see patients at a certain time during their pregnancy. I gave women the option of doing this, most of them decided to see me more often. This was frowned upon by managers but I felt more comfortable doing it. My ladies always came first with me.

One lady I had a lot to do with has in the last year had her 7th baby, she had her first baby in hospital and the others as home births. I delivered the 6 who were born at home; I think this is some sort of record and I am very proud of this. This couple lived on a farm with her parents. There was a long drive up to the house. Of course, I knew exactly where they lived, I had been there so often, but getting a 2nd midwife there in the middle of the night, which of course it always was proved to be more of a problem, but we managed it, sometimes more quickly than others.

I think this lady has finished having babies now and has a beautiful family who range from late teenage to one. They were a lovely family and they all lived in houses near to the parents. I went on to deliver two of the sister in laws three babies and was also there when her first baby was born; on a Christmas day in the hospital. I also looked after the other brother's wife when she had her two children; so knew my way to the farm very well.

I remember another family I had a fair amount to do with; lived in a village within my working area. I was the mother's midwife, and when her children grew up I was their midwife also. The house was not the cleanest and extremely cluttered.

The first time I went to the house to see the daughter, the parents proudly told me that they had decorated since I had last visited – well it was 18 years ago. To me it looked the same, this was a house that when you washed your hands you dried them on your cardigan, or waved them in the air, as the towels to say the least were unhealthy looking.

The now grandmother had put on quite a significant amount of weight since I had last seen her. She sat in her armchair with a large tin of biscuits on her lap. She had no teeth and was noisily sucking the biscuits; when she asked me if I would like one, I declined. The student who was with me was shocked at the house and the situation but it is something you have to get used to when working on community. It is smells that I find difficult.

I remember going to a house where the lady who lived there was a bank manager, so I was a little surprised to find the sofa was half eaten by a rather large dog; and its poo was all up the stairs. The smell was quite overpowering. I would not have let anyone in if I had lived there, but she was fine and obviously felt this was normal. We don't have much money but we do see life.

A colleague of mine went to see a lady who had just had her seventh baby. The 8-year-old daughter answered the door, telling her that her mum and dad were at the pub, and she was looking after the baby. Unbelievable. That was a case where social services were called and rightfully so.

A water birth I went to in Olney was a bit scary, the lady was quite a large person and she had elected to birth in the pool. When I arrived, she was five centimetres dilated so the pool was prepared and in she got. She was doing really well with the contractions but was bouncing from one side to the other side of the pool with each one.

At some point, the bottom section of the pool sprang a leak. The air was going out of it and the pool became very lop sided. The pool she had, had three sections so the other two were still blown up. I was worried that at some point, as she was doing her lurching, the water would flood the room and we would be unable to stop it. Just before she delivered the inevitable happened; the bottom of the pool collapsed. Fortunately, she was able to still deliver in the pool but we had to restrain her from leaping about. She managed to do this and all was well. I was never so pleased to see a baby. I thought we would be wading before it was born. Those pools hold a lot of water.

Chapter 21
My Dear Father Becomes Ill

Another sad time was coming in my life. My father had a stroke and was incapacitated for a time. By this time, he had married again and was being looked after by Iris, his wife, who had been one of my mum's best friends. Unfortunately, he soon had another stroke and had to be admitted to a nursing home. This was difficult for all of us. I remember one occasion. I had just been to my last visit. My daughter Charlotte rang me in a very upset state. She had gone to see her Pappy, but she could not find him in the communal lounge. She had been sent up to his bedroom where she had found him on the floor.

She called the staff and it turned out he had been on the floor all day. As you can imagine, we were all extremely upset by this, he had not hurt himself but was obviously very upset. My dad decided that he did not want this to happen again, so we had a meeting with the staff and he asked them if he could have a cot side put onto his bed. We all thought this was a good idea, but to our amazement the staff were not in agreement and said it infringed his civil liberties. We argued that it was what he wanted. Unfortunately, this fell on deaf ears and we got nowhere.

Soon after this, my poor dad had another stroke so was admitted to hospital. He was not there long before he died. The feeling of loss was awful. I remember saying to Richard, I feel like an orphan. Being without both parents is dreadful. You come to know that life is not infinite, also that you are the older ones now.

Going back to work after my father's death, I found very hard. I have been so lucky to work in a supportive surgery, with colleagues who look out for you. My children found it very difficult to get over his death but we all supported one another. Time does heal but you never forget losing a loved one.

Another house I remember well, was in the same village as the lady before. It was a lady in her early twenties and her partner. I met them at the surgery but did not visit them at home until they had delivered their baby. The house was quite dark. It had several interesting things on the wall of the sitting room, including metal chastity belts, and swords. I met my match when I went into the kitchen to wash my hands. They had a tarantula in a cage next to the sink, and small cages from floor to ceiling with rats in. I could not get out quickly enough it made me shudder. Each to his own.

Chapter 22
Water Births

When water births came into fashion I was a bit sceptical. I had a lady who wanted a water birth and I was very honest with her telling her I had never done one. I had read lots about them and watched videos, that's not the same as doing them. We had a manager who had done a lot of these at her previous hospital, so we arranged for us both to be in attendance.

When the time came the lady laboured in the pool and we all waited patiently for her to deliver. She was doing well and had her husband and her parents with her. Each time she had a contraction her father would say, come on darling you can do it. It was getting slightly wearing when thank goodness, she started pushing.

When the head delivered, the baby had its eyes wide open and was looking around as if to say what just happened. The baby was finally delivered and I remember saying to my manager under my breath, is the baby usually that colour; it seemed a bit blue. She told me this was normal that they soon change to pink.

We found out soon after that the baby had a heart defect which was a bit of a shock, but fortunately the heart defect was not too serious. After this delivery, I was hooked, water birth was the way to go and I have since delivered many women in the pool with no problems with their birth.

The only problem I have had, is when I had a student who was quite short. She reached down into the pool to guide the baby through the lady's legs and I nearly lost her over the side. I just managed to grab her before she took a nose dive. Also, a husband who wanted to get into the pool in his birthday suit!

This man was one of my own lady's husbands and had brought up the idea of getting into the pool in the nude, at the antenatal classes which I ran. I told him I did not think this was appropriate and said I was happy for him to get in the pool; but to wear swimming trunks. He vetoed this idea, and in the end, I had to say that I thought that it would be an insult to the midwife in charge of the delivery. He was not having no for an answer, so I asked him to ring the delivery suite sister to ask for her permission. He did this and she felt the same as me and told him it would not be allowed. The outcome of this delivery was, he got in the pool in his trunks, but jumped out when she was pushing and had a small bowel movement. Hilarious.

As community midwives, we still went into the hospital first thing in the morning. We had several offices some were fine, some not so good. The last office we had was lead lined so none of our mobiles worked in there. It got extremely hot especially in the summer. This was a little annoying as patients knew we were in the office at that time and tried to contact us. As we left to go about our calls, the phone would be ringing with messages. Charges for the car park were also a bone of contention; by the time I retired, I was paying nearly £13 a month for the pleasure of being in the office for an hour 8 times a month.

One winter's day when it was pouring with rain, I was asked to visit a lady who had delivered her baby. She belonged to the circus that was in the area. Off I went and found the field they were in. I was asked by some of the members of the circus to drive to the far side of the field, which I did. I found the caravan and the lady and her baby were very well. The problem came when I went to leave to go to my next visit. My car had sunk in the mud, and there was no way I was going to drive it out.

Some of the circus people gathered around, told me to get into my car and they would lift me out. Well, I was a bit reluctant but they assured me it would be fine. In the car I got. At that point, I rang my manager as I was running late for a clinic so I could ask if there was anyone that could go and start it for me. I was speaking to her when all of a sudden, the car was raised in the air. I shrieked as four men in the front and two elephants at the back lifted me up, I told my manager what was happening and she was shrieking with laughter. At the time it was not funny, but later I saw the funny side of it all.

I was able to drive out of the field but my car was absolutely filthy. That was something that did not happen very often.

Elephant's, and clowns helping out the midwife. Eventually, I made it to my clinic and when I told them what had happened they were hysterical. I do wish I had a video of it.

Chapter 23
Losing a Baby

Not all parts of a midwife's job are happy or funny, there are also sad times. The loss of a baby is a shattering thing to happen to a couple, and they need a lot of support. Midwives are there for this and it can be difficult and draining but so necessary. I have had several patients who have lost babies either in pregnancy, as a stillbirth, or after birth. I have tried hard to support these women and hope I have succeeded. I am still in touch with several of these ladies, most have gone on to have other children successfully and I have delivered several of their babies.

One of these ladies I remember especially, her first child was born, and it wasn't until then that we knew there was a problem. The baby failed to breathe spontaneously and was intubated at birth, then transferred to Oxford, which is a Centre of Excellence. The baby lived for several days, but unfortunately died aged 9 days. It was an extremely difficult time, as Christmas was around the corner, and when everyone is celebrating the birth of Jesus; it must have been so hard for them.

Around two years later, I got the much longed for news she was pregnant and obviously extremely nervous. This lady had a normal pregnancy and I promised I would be with her for the birth of her baby. All her scans showed that her baby was fine and I supported her as much as I could throughout her pregnancy.

When the call came it was decided I would go to her home. She would decide if she wanted to deliver at home or go to the hospital. She decided to birth at home and did really well. Her husband was so nervous it was awful not to be able to reassure him. He spent a lot of time in the garden smoking and pacing. The baby was eventually delivered and was absolutely fine. It was such a special time and both parents were so pleased they had stayed at home. It is so special to be able to do this for a couple and I feel so happy to have been a part of their special birth.

Car Accident

On a Saturday when working I had just done my last visit and thank goodness it was time to go home. My bladder was full, I was hungry, and five minutes from home. A Car, two cars in front of me, had stopped so he could turn right. I also stopped. The next minute, I was hit from behind. My head hit the windscreen, I was shot back into my seat. The air bag failed to go off. I sat in my seat thinking, "Oh god, I am still alive."

Unfortunately, I was pushed into the car in front of me and he hit the car in front of him so in all it was a 5-car smash. I was really shocked but managed to phone my husband. He left the house immediately making his way to where I was. His first comment was. I was just about to enjoy the Grand National.

The ambulance and police arrived and I was carted off to hospital, it was at this point I found out how uncomfortable it is to be lying flat of your back with your neck restrained in the back of an ambulance. All I could think of was I really needed the loo! Fortunately, I was not seriously hurt and returned home later in the day with a neck brace on, a sore back and, fortunately, an empty bladder.

This accident put me on the sick for 4 months. I found it a real struggle to get back in a car to drive. My car had been written off and for a while I was very nervous behind the wheel. I drove myself to the doctor's surgery 6 weeks after my accident. Without my knowledge my daughter, Emma followed me to make sure I made it.

During my consultation, my GP took my blood pressure, looked at me and said I think we need to take that when you have calmed down, it is through the roof. Driving got easier as time went on and after what seemed like an age I returned to work. That's when I knew my back would never be the same again. I didn't know how draining a bad back is.

When I started doing on calls again, I was honest with patients that I found it difficult to grovel about on the floor. I remember with clarity going to a home birth with a patient who wanted to deliver on all fours on the floor. I asked her if she would mind being on all fours on the sofa as my back wasn't brilliant. "Well, that's your problem," she said, "you are paid to deliver me so get on with it." This was unusual most ladies are great. I will deliver them in any position as long as I can get to them safely, women deliver in all sorts of places – half way up the stairs, in the bathroom, in the kitchen. It usually works out fine. I did manage to deliver this lady but it was a very difficult to be put in that position.

A memory from when I returned after my accident was chatting to the Health Visitor about what had happened whilst I had been off. She told me about one of the ladies who had miscarried at 16wks with twins. It was an IVF pregnancy and very much wanted. I knew this lady from when I had looked after her when she had her first baby. I asked the Health Visitor if she thought it would be alright for me to ring her; to see if she was coping alright. The Health Visitor thought the lady would like this, so I duly rang her after I had finished my clinic. The poor girl was so upset I offered to visit on my way home, which she said she would like.

I duly went to see her and heard about what had happened and how she felt about it. She went on to tell me that not one of the midwives had rung her to ask her if she was ok. She had felt that no one had acknowledged her loss, and that no one had cared.

I must admit that I was quite shocked and upset that this had not been done, but obviously it was too late to put it right. I visited this lady on several occasions, and thankfully she became pregnant a few months later, and without any interventions.

This lady was so anxious during this pregnancy that I visited as often as I could. Fortunately, the pregnancy went well, and she delivered a beautiful baby girl. I am still in contact with this lady, and we are now firm friends. In fact, she has just delivered her 3rd baby. The moral of this tale is that midwives need to keep up to date with what is happening with their women and let them know they care.

Chapter 24
Doulas

One delivery I remember with humour is a lady who wanted a water birth with a doula in tow. When I arrived at the house she gave me her birth plan which was a revelation. I had to sit down to read and digest it. She had lots of rules and regulations: Firstly, no one was to look at her lady bits; we were not to cheer lead her; not to feed her pasta, the list went on. It was quite comical, and we went through each point and reached a compromise.

Her doula was a bit of a nightmare; she was Irish with hair that stuck up in a big frizzy mess. She had never seen a birth before and was still in her training. Some of the doulas comments were a bit odd. She had no idea how to calm the patient; but was convinced she was going to deliver the baby. I do wonder if she ever passed her course to become a doula.

The lady was in the pool and, of course, we had to take the temperature of the water and keep it to a comfortable heat for her and safe for her baby. There was no hot water available in the house so we were boiling kettles, saucepans and anything we could find to do this. When we had done this numerous times; the kettle stopped working. We had to send the doula to Tesco at 2am to get a new one. We had to have a whip round to fund this venture, thinking about it I never got my money back.

I called the 2nd midwife, when the lady was 8cm, and I remember well sitting on the bottom step of the stairs with the other midwife pointing out the titles of some of the books on the bookshelf. That was a bit of a revelation, I didn't know you could buy such books!

At one point, during her birth, her partner wanted to use the little boy's room but she wasn't having it. She was in pain so he could suffer too. We did tell her that this was a bit silly as he couldn't support her if he was bursting. She did eventually let him go and relieve himself. She did deliver as she wanted in the pool; unfortunately, we had to look at her lady bits to facilitate this; but we promised we would not remember what we had seen.!!

Having students is part of a midwife's role. I always enjoyed teaching the next generation of midwives. I remember one student I had who suffered from car sickness. I worked in the area furthest away from the hospital many of my ladies lived in small villages so driving was part of the job.

This poor girl was sick time and time again. I was forever stopping the car to let her vomit. I felt really sorry for her but it was impeding my job. It's the only time I have asked managers if I could change my student so she could work in a smaller area so would not be so indisposed, and I could work as I was supposed to. My wish was granted and I often wonder what happened to this girl, I don't think she would ever be able to work on community unless she had a very small area or got over her sickness problems.

She also had some very weird ideas about childbirth. I had to ask her to refrain from her comments in one ante natal class as she was telling the ladies that no one needed pain relief, it was not necessary, and they should not go down this road. I did say to her: "When you have your own children you can do as you like. I am giving women the information they need to make an informed choice. Pain relief should be a choice, women should not feel guilty because they need or want it."

One home birth I attended was in a house where building work was being carried out. The only toilet in the house was in the main bedroom and had no door on it! The lady was having her second baby and thankfully was progressing very well. The husband kept plying me with cups of tea, which usually I would be very grateful for, but knowing the toilet arrangements I was holding back. The time came to call the second midwife and thankfully the lady delivered quite soon after she arrived. By this time, my bladder was round my neck. When you're desperate for the loo and you have to wee in front of all, it's a bit of a put off; but needs must. By the time I had been there for 6 hours, there was no holding back. Just shut your eyes, perform and carry on with the delivery. This was a lovely delivery, lovely couple but I was so pleased when it was over. It is surprising what the difference a door makes.

Chapter 25
Baby Born Before Midwife Gets There

Many years ago, I was called to a BBA (baby already born) in a student house. It was a freezing night. I found the girl was in a room with no carpets, it was cold and unwelcoming. The baby was wrapped in a towel in her mother's arms. It was decided we should take her into hospital as she said she had not known she was pregnant, had no baby equipment or nappies and the house was cold. The baby was in good condition as was the mum; so she was taken by ambulance to the delivery ward. I followed in my car.

She had two gentlemen with her and I left them in the waiting area whilst we made the mother comfortable. A little time later, I asked the mother who she wanted in with her, and she said just the father of the baby. I went to the waiting area and requested that the father of the baby should follow me. That is when it got slightly difficult, both men stood up and followed me, so I reiterated just the father, they both replied we are the father, so we all went into the room and I left them too it. I later found out that the mother was actually saying she did not know who the father was but decided as she did not know she was pregnant she would have the baby adopted.

One evening, I had a lady in my area that wanted a home birth. It was before we had 2nd midwives with us. The local GP who was great, knew this lady very well, and told me to call him when she was ready for delivery and he would come and assist. The lady progressed very well and I called the GP who duly arrived. I had the room set out for the delivery with the oxygen and suction in an area in case it was needed to help the baby breathe.

The GP asked me what I needed from him and I told him everything was ok at the moment; but I pointed out the oxygen and suction. The lady delivered shortly after that and as I was delivering her, I looked to the GP. He was reading the instructions on the equipment. It was hilarious but, thankfully, was not needed as the baby cried spontaneously and lustfully. I often teased him about this event and he took it all in good faith. I don't think the lady saw him doing it but the husband certainly did and his face was a picture.

Chapter 26
I Didn't Know I Was Pregnant

I have always found it incredible and difficult to believe when a woman does not know she is pregnant. One lady, I did believe was the talk of the hospital. This lady was suffering from stomach pains and had been to see her GP several times. The last GP she saw decided that she should go the Accident and Emergency department, as he thought she may have kidney stones.

When she arrived at the hospital and had been given a scan it was found that she was actually pregnant and was having contractions. When I heard this story, I could not believe four doctors had missed her pregnancy. When I met her; I understood.

This lady was enormous. She had probably not seen any difference in her abdominal girth. She had put her pains and the movements down to indigestion.

I had the pleasure of visiting her when she got home with her baby. Her husband (who was a tiny chap) and her had been trying for a baby for 8years and were so delighted with their beautiful baby. I remember vividly sitting on one end of the three-seater settee. When the mum sat down her lap was on my lap.

A colleague of mine had visited the day before and told me to look at the beautiful picture above the fireplace. Well of course I looked. It was a photograph of their wedding. The lady had on a huge puffy dress. It reminded me of the loo roll holders that people used to have. Just a head on a marquee, it was difficult trying not to laugh.

They were a really nice couple who actually went on to have another child. That time she knew she was pregnant. I saw this lady several years later with her eldest child and she was still enormous. The little girl was an absolute replica of her, but a happier family you couldn't find.

One morning when I was going into the main entrance of the hospital, I saw a lady getting out of a taxi, she looked pale and seemed to be struggling. As I was the only one around, I asked if I could help. She told me that the delivery suite was expecting her. I took her suitcase and helped her to the lift. In the lift, we chatted and she said she had had her baby in the night. I asked where the baby was and she told me as we arrived on the delivery suite. "Oh, it is in the suitcase!"

I sat her in the reception area and I hurried down to the desk, stating that I need a room now and a senior midwife. The staff all looked at me as if I had lost the plot; I just said, "Baby in suitcase." The lady was taken into the room and the baby was retrieved from the suitcase. It was cold and limp and I really thought it was dead, but when it was lifted out I saw the baby was breathing. Within seconds a neonatal doctor was in the room, and the neonatal nurses had arrived. I don't know who was most shocked, me or the midwife who came into the room with me.

The mother did not seem at all concerned about what was going on and was asking for a cup of tea. The baby was taken into the neonatal unit and, fortunately, did very well and went on to be adopted. That's a delivery I will never forget. I do not know what happened to the lady I know she was admitted to the ward but if any charges were brought against her I don't know.

Chapter 27
Snowy Nights

One icy snowy night I was called out to attend a home birth in a little village not far from my home. I drove very slowly as the roads were awful and found I could not get to the house because of the snow. I called the lady and she told me to hang on; her husband would come and get me. Several minutes later, a tractor arrived. On I got and was driven to the house, freezing cold from my journey but glad to have arrived at my destination.

The lady was having good contractions and coping very well. The hours went by and eventually it was time to call the second midwife. I phoned the delivery suite and told them the situation, asking them to tell the midwife to ring me when she reached the village, and the husband would fetch her.

The 2nd midwife on call was an Italian girl, really nice, but quite dramatic in her ways. We got the phone call and off went the dad to pick her up. Her face was a picture when she arrived. She had never been on the back of a tractor before and could talk of nothing else. Thankfully, the delivery went well and the baby was born with no problem.

The escape route from the house was the same as when we arrived. The back of the tractor. When we reached at our cars, we needed a spade and a lot of deicer to get our cars going. I was extremely pleased to get home safely.

This lady went on to have more children which I delivered; but never in such bad weather. The lady lived in Dubai and came home to her mums to have her children. Her husband worked for the foreign office, and they paid for the deliveries so it worked very well. This lady had 3 more babies and I managed to deliver them all.

In the community office one morning, we had a notification that a lady had delivered her baby at a private hospital in London. She lived on a farm not far from where I lived, so I was asked to do the visit. I was presented with a very long drive at the top of which was a five-bar locked gate, by the side of which was a button to press. I pressed the button stated I was the midwife, and the gate was raised so I drove in.

I got to the door and a lady with a baby in her arms answered. I introduced myself and she asked me in a very posh voice, are you private or National Health. I informed her I worked for the National Health Service and her reply was – well piss off then. So, I did.

I rang the manager to tell her what had happened and she rang the lady who told her she wanted a private midwife. One of our consultants had a retired midwife working for him in his private clinic, so it was arranged for this lady to visit.

I got a phone call from this midwife asking me what she needed to do, when the baby's blood test was due; oh and could she borrow my scales. I gave the information she needed plus the form for the baby's blood test and wondered what the patient thought she was paying for. The midwife phoned me from her house several times to ask my opinion, and they paid her £75 a visit!! I found out later that when the GP had visited he was seen off the premises with a shot gun. I think I got off lightly.

Chapter 28
Becoming a Nana

My youngest daughter was the first of my children to get pregnant. She did it with a plus. She was expecting identical twins, how exciting and scary. She was looked after at the hospital where I worked and she and her husband were very excited.

They were lucky enough to be sent to London for special scans and we found that they were identical. Fortunately, there was a membrane separating them, so she was lucky as this can help to stop some difficulties that come with such twins. Her pregnancy went well until she was 32 weeks when she was found to have developed eclampsia.

This is a dangerous complication of pregnancy and it was decided when she was 33 weeks she needed to be delivered. I went into theatre with her for an emergency C-section not knowing if she was having boys or girls. Our family only had girls it seemed, so I was delighted when they turned out to be boys. Edward was delivered first quickly followed by George; the most gorgeous babies I have ever seen, although I could be a bit biased. They were taken to the neonatal unit shortly after their birth and thankfully did very well.

I was the chief photographer, so was busy with the camera but found it very difficult watching the consultant cutting my daughter. I was privileged that they wanted me there. Emma went home 5 days later, but unfortunately had complications. She was readmitted with a paralytic ileus. (the bowel does not work). This is a rare but nasty complication of abdominal surgery. Emma was put in a side room and had intravenous fluids, a naos gastric tube in her nose and was really poorly for a while.

I remember going in to see her one morning and she sat in a chair with a drip in each hand plus a tube up her nose; trying to express milk for her babies, crying because she could not get any. "Just stop this," I told her. You have not eaten for 5 days, you have no milk and at this point your babies need you more than they need your milk.

It was a very difficult time for a while but eventually she got better and was able to look after her babies. The boys came home when they were 3 weeks old on Boxing Day and they went from strength to strength. They are now 11; nearly 12 and doing very well. The only problem they have is that their eye sight is a little down and they both wear glasses. They are bright intelligent boys who are doing very well at school. They have both just been made prefects. We are so proud of them.

Charlotte my eldest daughter was the next to bless us with a grandchild. We were so thrilled for her and her partner Justin when we heard the news.

I looked after Charlotte throughout her pregnancy and it went very smoothly. Unfortunately, she went very overdue so was booked in for induction. I so wanted to deliver her and got the call at 3am to say she was in full blown labour. I drove to the hospital and met Justin in the car park, so we arrived together.

Charlotte coped very well and was in the pool for a while, but unfortunately her little one was in no hurry to arrive. She reached full dilatation, after over an hour of pushing it was evident that she needed some help. The cavalry was called, and a lovely doctor and midwife arrived who immediately took control and helped bring the baby into the world. I didn't get to deliver her but it was a joy to be there to support her, although I was a blubbing mess by the time our gorgeous granddaughter Evee arrived.

I had sent Charlotte for a scan at 34 weeks as I thought the baby was small, but they estimated that she was 6lbs at that scan so I stopped worrying. Evee was 6lbs 1oz at birth so I think the scan was a bit out, but she was healthy that was the main thing.

Charlotte then had to go to theatre to have the placenta delivered as it was stuck. So, she went to theatre and I went home to bed, exhausted but delighted. I sneaked Justin's parents into the delivery suite so that they could support Justin whilst Charlotte was in theatre.

Evee is now 4 years old and such a darling, I look after her one day a week whilst Charlotte works. She is an absolute delight, we have great fun. We went conker picking last week and she proudly showed her grandad her honkers, the new word for conkers. I keep asking her if she would like a brother or sister but she very politely tells me no thank you.

Maternity Care Assistants

The introduction of maternity care assistants seemed odd to us midwives. We couldn't see how they could help us. How wrong we were. I have worked with a lot of them and most of them are great. They work so hard and have helped enormously with the midwife's workloads.

They are very professional ladies who enhance the work of the midwife. My opinion is they need a pay rise. They take on a lot of the pressure off the midwives; they help with breast feeding, babies blood tests, support the mothers who need it and are an integral part of the team. They do a lot of the answering of the phones, also take on a lot of the dreaded paperwork. Another skill they excel in is helping at ante natal classes, this takes a lot of pressure off the midwives, and we found it an enormous help.

Working in a small place means that you are known by most of the population. When the girls were little we used to go the local market, but the girls got fed up with us being stopped. They used to count how many times we spoke to people. It also can make for amusing encounters.

I was in the local supermarket one day after work, when I met a lady who had had a lot of problems with her stiches healing after her birth. She had a gorgeous son of about 3; who used to call me 'the baby doctor'. He saw me and shouted very loudly up the aisle, "Are you going to look at my mum's bum today?" The mother's face was a picture, it was so funny; good job people knew who I was.

We had so many good midwives and one I really enjoyed working with was from the Caribbean. She was an absolute star and always up for a laugh. I had been called out to a birth and she was second on call, so as the woman progressed I rang her and along she came. The woman wanted to birth on all fours on the floor which was fine.

The second midwife sat on a chair waiting for the woman to deliver, and laughing, every time she had a contraction and pushed, the lady moved around the room and I followed her, with my delivery pack beside me. We went around and round that living room. It was hilarious, it's a wonder I didn't have a hole in the knee of my trousers from all the movement, but eventually she delivered and the roundabout came to a halt.

Chapter 29
Other Ways of Working

Not all midwives work in the same way as their colleagues. I did some visits for a midwife who was on a day off and was quite shocked by what I found. The first lady was very tearful when I visited her. I had a chat and asked her about her worries. This lady proceeded to tell me that she was having problems with her left breast and she had been diagnosed with breast cancer. I asked how and when she had found this out this news. She said the midwife who came yesterday told her because she had a lump on her breast. I asked if the GP had been informed of her problem, she said she didn't think so! I asked if I could examine her breast, and if necessary ask the GP for advice.

She allowed me to examine her, and I could see that she had mastitis (an infection in the breast.). It was red and inflamed and was very painful. I informed the lady I needed to ring the GP to get her some antibiotics and the problem would be solved. It was a quite upsetting event and I reassured her that midwives did not diagnose breast cancer. It is not in our field of expertise, and that the GP was going to visit her at the end of his surgery. I left a very different lady when I eventually left her house.

The next patient who had been visited by the same midwife told me she had a uterine infection and was on antibiotics, but she didn't feel any different since taking the tablets. I asked to examine her abdomen and she agreed. I palpated her uterus which was not tender, asking her when she had last had her bowels open. She had a think and then said, "Not since I had the baby." The baby was 8 days old.

I asked if she had seen her GP and she told me she had not and that the midwife had rung him. She had no other symptom of an infection, normal temperature and no tenderness. With her permission, I administered glycerine suppositories. The outcome was excellent. I feel much better now she told me. I was quite shaken by what I had seen, so I was a bit worried about my next visit.

The third lady was sitting very gingerly and complaining of severe perineal pain. (Pain in her stitch area.) This lady had had a forceps delivery and an episiotomy. She told me the midwife had looked at her the day before and told her it was fine. As I had had problems with this midwife's care I asked to view it for myself.

This poor lady had a completely broken-down episiotomy which had not happened overnight. It was very infected, red and sore looking. I rang the GP, told him I had taken a swab, and asked him for his advice. She was given antibiotics and was very grateful. These three visits had left me in a difficult position. *Do I just ignore what I had witnessed or say something?*

I decided that I couldn't leave it. I decided to have a word with the midwife's supervisor, who then had a meeting with her. She did some visits with her to assess her care.

I felt really bad that this midwife was taken off community and was brought back into the hospital for updating. Thankfully, she never knew it was me that had told the management but I feel I did the right thing, the patients care is paramount and they deserve the best from all midwives.

Another midwife also gave me cause for concern. I was working a weekend and was not on call but had a call from a colleague one morning, to ask me to join her at a home birth. When I arrived, she was with a lady who was in early labour. I wondered why she had called me. It turned out she had no child care and her four children were in the car outside the house.

She asked me to take the children on my rounds with me. I was quite shocked but told her I felt unable to do this as they were quite unruly, also I did not have the appropriate car seats and had a lot of visits to do. I felt it was not the right thing to do. I told her I would look after this lady if she took the visits.

This did not go down very well as she wanted to deliver the lady. It turned out she always had her children with her at the weekend, as she had no child care. It put me in a really difficult position. In the end, I drove the children to my house, and my husband looked after them. I did tell her that this was not professional and that she needed to sort out her child care. I arrived home at 5pm to find the children still there. The lady had delivered, but the midwife had some shopping to do so had not yet picked them up.

I was not amused. I told her that it was not fair on the children to be left in a car for hours on end whilst she did her job. Now I knew why I was always getting called to do visits that were missed. When five o'clock came around she turned her phone off so any visits she had not done, had to be phoned out to other midwives. I was told soon after this event that she had taken a Head of Midwifery job in Dubai. I hope she had more support for her children whilst she was doing this job.

This reminds me of a lady of mine, that I visited, who was deaf. She had delivered before she reached the hospital; had been checked over by the midwife and then sent home. She was telling me that she felt very sore down below and I asked her if she would like me to have a look for her.

I was so shocked. I was looking at the lady's vagina. She had a fourth-degree tear (a tear that goes all the way through the rectum). I had never seen one before; but had no doubt that this was what had happened. Unfortunately, her husband was out at the time of my visit, so I rang the hospital and spoke to the consultant on call in the Delivery suite and explained what I had found.

I turned my back on the lady so she could not lip read what I was saying, so I did not distress her. The consultant knew me well and just said, send her in, it is probably not a fourth-degree tear, but we will have a look.

I explained to the lady what was happening and asked if I could phone her husband; so that he could take her to the hospital. I waited for the husband to return and explained to him what I had found. He was quite cross and obviously wanted to know why it wasn't found at the hospital. A very difficult question to answer.

It turned out on questioning that the midwife had not looked to see if she had torn. The outcome of this event was that the lady did have a 4th degree tear, so was taken to theatre and sutured. She was in hospital for several days and had many problems later on with her bowels leaking. It was so sad, but hopefully in time it would improve.

These tears are best sutured as soon as possible after the birth. This lady had hers for more than twenty-four hours before it was stitched. They moved house shortly after the baby was born, so I did not find out the final outcome, but I do hope she has improved, as this sort of problem for a young mum or for anyone is devastating.

Chapter 30
Managers

Don't get me going on managers; we were overrun with them. We have specialist midwives in so many things these days. Child protection, breast feeding, diabetes, teenage pregnancy, mental health, you name it we have it. All very necessary but I feel deskilling the midwives who work with the patients. None of these midwife's work weekends and surprise the community girls cope.

What with the head of midwifery, 3 modern matrons, 3 team leaders, and a consultant midwife, that's an awful lot of very skilled good midwives sitting in an office. I do know things need to move on but do query if this is the way to do it. The latest thing is a home birth team, looking after all the women who want a home birth. Well, if one of my ladies wants a home birth I wanted to look after her and hopefully deliver her.

Our hospital ran a service a few years ago for midwives in a team to look after a selection of women who they saw through their pregnancies and then delivered them and visiting them after their birth. A wonderful service but couldn't be kept up. The midwives were on their knees and the service was stopped. Next thing we hear: it is starting again as the way forward. Managers seem to have short memories.

All these ideas that they came up with. Maybe, if they had to work in these teams they would know, it is not the way forward.

On one occasion, one of the so called expert midwives was called into delivery suite to help as they were short staffed. She delivered the lady and the placenta but felt unable to suture the woman and needed help. This is one of the midwives who are teaching all the other midwives how to do such procedures. It is not the same suturing two pieces of foam together as it is suturing skin on a moving patient. Maybe, these midwives should have to work in the real world on a regular basis to keep up their skills before they teach the rest of us.

It is very difficult to get into midwifery these days. In fact, if I were starting my working life again I would not get on the course. I have not got A levels so would not have been accepted. I have had a good career and worked well as a midwife. I do wonder if the profession is losing out on girls who have the passion for midwifery but not the qualifications. I don't mean we need girls with no qualifications; I also don't think you need a degree to be a midwife; just common sense, a love of the job and able to work effectively and safely with patients and managers.

The Prof

One of my favourite people I worked with was a consultant. He was charming, clever and excellent at his job. I ran clinics with him for many years at my surgery and had the greatest respect for him.

One night I was called into the unit to help as they were very busy. I was directed to a room in which a lady was having her second baby. She had had a C-section with her first child because he had been in the breech position but was desperate to have a normal birth with this baby.

I had a chat with them both and the night went on with her progressing very well, until she was fully dilated. Although, she was fully dilated she had no urge to push, so I told her to carry on as she was doing well. She was fine and baby was happy, we should wait for the urge to push. Both she and her husband were happy with this.

Then a knock at the door; and a registrar appeared for an update. I gave him a resume of what was happening, and he told the lady that he wanted to examine her. If you are fully dilated you should be pushing. The poor woman looked at me and told the doctor that she did not want to be examined again and wanted a chance to deliver normally. The doctor proceeded to tell her she was putting her baby at risk; and after a few minutes of this, I tried to intervene to persuade the doctor to let her continue as she was doing so well. I was more or less told I was putting the woman at risk, so I excused myself from the room and went to the desk where I told the staff that I was going to ring the consultant. I was told that I could do that, just watch me I said. I rang the consultant gave him a run down on what was happening. He listened and said I will be there as soon as I can.

I returned to the room to a very distressed lady who was pleading with the doctor to let her continue. This was not going to happen so I intervened and told them that, "The consultant was coming in to discuss this with them, so don't fret all is going well."

Oh dear, the registrar was obviously furious and asked me to go out of the room with him which I duly did. He was outraged that I had dared you go above him. "I am in charge of the Delivery ward tonight and you will do as I say."

I replied, "I am sorry but intervention at this point is not necessary, I want the woman to have a normal birth."

Fortunately, at that point the consultant arrived and asked me to take him into the room to introduce him to the mother. He looked at the woman and told her, you are doing great, carry on. I will sit in the corner so that I am here if you need me. Talk about the cavalry arriving, it was so good of him to come in.

A few minutes later, the lady said she needed to push; so, after pushing for just under an hour her beautiful baby arrived. The consultant got to his feet, shook the woman and her husband's hands, said, "Well done," and left the room. He left a very happy couple in the room and after the after-birth was delivered and mum was comfortable. I went out to the desk, not really knowing what I would face with the registrar.

I got to the desk to hear the consultant saying to the registrar, "If Carol tells you to do something do it. She has more experience with normal births than you will ever have." Woops, I was slightly embarrassed but so pleased for the couple.

The same consultant was on duty when I took my sister in law Susie in to deliver her second baby. She already had a girl who I had seen delivered but was hopefully going to be able to deliver this child for her. She was doing really well but was feeling very hot and bothered; so she flung off her nightie and was walking around the room stark naked, puffing on the gas and air, with me one side and her husband Peter on the other side.

At that very moment, there was a knock at the door and the consultant walked in, shook her by the hand, told her she was

100

doing well and left the room. Her face was a picture, she has never forgotten it. It was very funny and we often bring it up and have a laugh about it. It was a great to be able to deliver William.

I have always felt a special rapport with Suzie. She now had a daughter, Claudia; I had been at her delivery but she needed help from the doctors and now a son, who I did deliver: so a pigeon pair.

This consultant, we will call him Prof, was the one I had called when Emma had been ill during her pregnancy. He had been looking after Emma throughout her pregnancy and had been brilliant. I called him from the ward, he told me not to worry: tell them not to do anything until he got there.

He arrived on the ward a few hours later, took one look at Emma and said right we need get these babies out. He delivered them himself. I found out later that he had been on holiday with his family in Wales and had come back especially for her. I was so grateful to him but felt really bad, his words where it is not a problem, I am going back tonight. What a star.

Mufti

A new rule was coming in for community midwives. We no longer needed to wear uniforms if we did not want to. I carried on wearing mine as I found it more professional. I don't have to think every work day what to wear. I don't know whether it's a good idea wearing mufti, some of the younger midwives I thought did not look professional, showing tattoos etcetera but some of the outfits were more like they were going to the club, not to work.

So, another rule came in. You can wear mufti but no jeans and you have to look professional. I have been into work in mufti, but not very often, I always seemed to get weed or pooped on when I don't wear uniform. The other thing I feel is wrong about no uniforms is you cannot tell who is a midwife, a student, or a health-care assistant unless you look at their name tags. I also believe that tattoos should not be on show as it is not very professional. Perhaps, I am just old and a bit set in my ways.

I remember vividly a lady I booked for her pregnancy. She was a young mum, very sweet, and had her boyfriend with her. He was very full of his own importance. The first thing he said to me was, "She has a tin plate in her head." It turned out she had had a brain tumour as a child and part of her skull bone had been replaced with a titanium plate.

Throughout the booking appointment, he kept chipping in, not letting her speak for herself, so I turned my chair so I was directly opposite her. He didn't like that at all. When we got to his details he was very quick to tell me he couldn't work as he had a bad back. He was 21 and had never had a job. The girl worked full time, so I said, "Well, you will be a house husband then and be in charge of looking after the baby." He quickly told me he would not be able to do this as his back was awful.

Later on, in her pregnancy, I went into the surgery late on a Friday afternoon, to find the receptionist in tears. It turned out this girl's partner had rung the surgery asking for a repeat prescription. When he was told it would not be ready until after the weekend, he had been extremely rude telling the receptionist that he would be admitted to hospital with the pain, if she didn't sort it out for him, it would be her fault.

I happened to be going to visit this lady on my way home so asked if I could help. It turned out his prescription was for Paracetamol and Gaviscon. (Which is for heartburn.) I told the receptionist not to worry. I would try to have a word with him.

When I reached the house, he proceeded to tell me how useless the surgery was, that they should understand that he needed his pain killers. My reply was, "Is it that urgent? What is the prescription for?"

He told me.

I asked him why he did not go and buy some from the chemist. "I will have to pay for them," he said, "my prescriptions are free." Well, the rule is you need to ask for a prescription 48hrs before you need it.

It turned out that he had not got a diagnosis for his back complaint. He had been sent to several different hospitals who all gave the same diagnosis. Nothing abnormal detected. His reply to this was all doctors are useless.

My advice for this chap, try getting a job then you will not have time to think about your 'bad back'. Some people just don't help themselves. I know a bad back is very draining; I myself saw a consultant a year after my car crash, who told me that I would not be working in 6 months. My back too was in a bad state. My husband, who was with me, asked me when we left the room, "What are you going to do?"

My reply, "I am going to carry on. If I stop working and moving, I will seize up." I kept working for 10yrs after this diagnosis. So, mind over matter does help, although, I did have to have back surgery 5 years ago and now have quite a lot of metalwork in my spine.

After I had back surgery, I was in intensive care, for 24hrs, and had a bad experience. I had an epidural in place for pain relief which was to be left in place for 48hrs. During the night, the nurse on duty was quite rough in her handling of me and seemed to shove me from side to side quite often and after a few of these turns, I started to feel pain. I told the nurse and she just said, "You cannot have pain; you have an epidural in place."

Fortunately for me, soon after this my daughter Emma arrived; took one look at me and said, "What on earth is the matter."

My reply, "The pain is unbearable. I don't know what to do with myself."

She left the ward and located the consultant at the desk and told him what was happening. He came back into the room and gently turned me onto my side to find out that the epidural had been pulled out, so I was not receiving the pain relief I needed.

He was not happy and called the nurse into the room telling her to get me some pain relief; she duly returned with tablets which I took, but they did not help. About half an hour later, I was crying in pain; so Emma left the ward again and fetched another nurse, who looked at my medication chart to find out I had been given Paracetamol. Fortunately for me, the right medication was given and the pain receded.

My motto is, *If a patient says they are in pain believe them, this includes women who are having contractions. They know how they feel, and if they say they want to push believe them, unless you can prove otherwise.*

It was difficult to return to work after my surgery. I had had a difficult recuperation, with infections, and pain. I actually got quite depressed, so was not my former self for quite a while. I remember going home after a particularly difficult day and saying to my husband, "I am not coping."

His reply was, "I know, but stick with it you will get there," and thankfully I did; with a lot of help from family and friends.

When I first returned to work, I was not doing on calls so missed doing my deliveries but, thankfully, I was able to take this back up again and return to being called out of my bed to deliver babies.

My first call out after a long time was to a couple who were having their 3rd baby. They had never had a home birth before but had decided that this is what they wanted for this baby. When I arrived at the house at 3am, I said to the husband, "I hope you have the kettle on."

He said, "No, how much water do we need."

"Just enough for a cup of tea" I said, Bless him. He so wanted to do everything right, he thought he had to boil the water for the birthing pool. "No," said I, "babies are not sterile, just fill it up from the tap."

The poor man had been boiling the kettle for hours to fill the pool; so was very relieved by my entrance. We all went into the lounge where his wife was pacing the room, desperate to get into the pool. I offered to examine her so she could get into the pool and she jumped at the chance. After examining her and checking the pool temperature, she was able to get in and heaved a sigh of relief.

The husband was quite anxious and asked me if we shouldn't be doing something. I replied, "We are listening in the baby's heart beat every 15min; checking the pool and mum's temperature on a regular basis, so let us just relax and let it happen."

"Well this is different from being in the hospital," he said. "She had been delivered at a consultant unit on previous occasions and been tied down by equipment so had felt out of control."

My answer to that was, "Everything is fine; both mum and baby are doing well so we will just leave her to get on with it."

He was relieved to hear this and calmed down and eventually thoroughly enjoyed the experience. The 2nd midwife was called and a beautiful normal birth was the outcome. We left a very happy mum and dad with their baby. They could not believe that the room was clear and it was all over. It's a wonderful feeling to be at a delivery like this and I cannot get enough of it.

One night, I was called to three different deliveries throughout the night and it was exhausting. The first delivery was a rapid one. I was called at 11pm and delivered the baby at 1am. Back to the hospital for refilling the bags and doing the computer work. Whilst, there was another call to a home birth; so I said to the second midwife, "Go home, try get some rest and I will call you if I need you."

I went off to the next birth and the 2nd midwife had 3 hours in bed before I called her again and we delivered another baby. Back to the hospital we went. Refilled the bags, filled in the paperwork and off home I went. I had not got into my bed before the next call came and off I went again.

By this time, I was exhausted and had now been on the go for 21hrs. When I arrived at the 3rd delivery, I was praying for a quick delivery, and fortunately this was to happen. I had to call the 2nd midwife again who was groaning by this point, but she arrived. We delivered the baby and decided that, as it was 8.30am now, it was time to call the cavalry and get someone to come and relieve us.

By the time the relief had come and I got into my car to go home, it was 10am. I was so exhausted I don't know how I drove home. I arrived home and after a short shower and quick breakfast, fell into my bed and slept like a baby. A busy night but in the end very satisfying to have delivered three babies.

One very warm evening I was called to another home birth. I picked up my student, Gill, on the way. When we arrived, the lady was in established labour, doing very well. It turned out she had not got anything ready for the birth, so we were hunting round for bin bags, towels, and baby clothes.

It was a small room we were in and extremely hot; so we opened the windows to try to get some air. It was the lady's 3rd baby and she progressed quite quickly. At one point, she got onto the bed and stated she wanted to push. So, I did what I always did, I looked to see if I could see the presenting baby. At that very point, she pushed; her waters went and I was doused in liquid from head to foot. My hair was dripping, much to amusement of Gill.

We went on to deliver the baby and all was well. It was still quite hot in the room and my dress was drying on me. It was awful; liquor is very sticky. I looked and felt a bit of a mess. Gill pointed out to me, she would have stood back when she looked and I think I she was right. Lesson learnt. I was glad to get home and get cleaned up but that was not until we had been back to the hospital to replenish the bags and do all the paperwork.

A delivery with a doula in tow can be great or it can be very trying. One lady wanted a home birth after a very difficult first birth, ending with an emergency C-section. Guess who got called – it always seemed to happen to me. It was a weekend daytime delivery which is quite unusual. It is usually in the middle of the night. When I arrived, she was pacing the room and coping quite well. She was reluctant to be examined, but allowed me to take her blood pressure, temperature and pulse and to listen to the heartbeat of the baby. She was very reluctant to have a vaginal examination so I thought we should get to know one another a bit better then maybe she would let me see how far dilated she was.

Her husband was sitting in the sun room, with 3 very large dogs, and said he could not leave them as they would react badly to strangers in the house. That was good to know! An hour or so later, she was finding the contractions difficult to deal with so I asked her if she would like to be examined so that I could give her some pain relief. Her doula was very vocal in her negative response to this, "No, that is not going to happen. We know she is progressing so just leave her alone. Maybe she had a crystal ball."

Unfortunately, I did not; so tried to explain about dilatation and how necessary it was to know that she was progressing.

This did not go down very well with the doula who told me, "Leave her alone. We are in full control."

I must admit I did not feel in control, as I knew from her history that she had not dilated beyond 3 centimetres with her first pregnancy. I had the knowledge from that delivery that the baby had been in distress and had spent some days in the intensive care unit. I tried to explain my worries to the mother who was still reluctant to be examined, so I kept my cool, as the baby and the mother seemed to be doing well and at this point so there was no need for intervention.

After I had been there for 4 hours, the lady started to have the sensation to push. So, I decided to send for the 2nd midwife, who arrived quite promptly. I went out to meet her and explained what was going on. She rolled her eyes and agreed with me that the lady needed examining. We decided to have a talk to the mum and dad and explain to them that we did not want her to push on a cervix that was not dilated as this could cause problems for her and the baby; and very reluctantly she agreed to this.

The doula still kept arguing with us, but I told her that the lady was giving her consent to an examination and that we were going ahead with this. We took the lady upstairs and asked the doula to stay downstairs. This was obviously not going to happen and she followed us upstairs.

The vaginal examination showed that the lady was 2cm dilated (she needed to get to ten) so this was not ideal. The cervix was also quite swollen where she had been pushing. We knew that this delivery unfortunately was not going to happen at home. The doula was not happy and kept telling us that this is not what she wants. "Well it was not what we want either," I told her, "but it would be dangerous to leave the lady at home as in time the baby would go into distress." This was not what we wanted at home.

After a long chat with the lady and her husband she agreed to be transferred to the hospital and an ambulance was called. This lady was taken into the delivery suite and the doula was with her. The doula informed the senior midwife that I obviously did not examine her correctly as she was more dilated than I had said and she was not happy. The lady accepted the need for another examination and the doula asked for a midwife or doctor who knew what they were doing to perform it!

The registrar on call was summoned, he examined her and, unfortunately, she was still 2cm. This poor lady did not want another C-section and was given pain relief; also time to dilate but, unfortunately, did not progress so was taken to theatre for a C-section some hours later. It is an awful shame when things don't go as well as wanted, but it can be quite stressful for the midwives dealing with it.

The eldest lady I have looked after was 53 and her husband was about the same. At the time I was excited that I had a lady who was older than me. They were both retired head teachers and had been waiting for a baby for over 20years. This pregnancy was made possible by in vitro fertilization, and they were thrilled to be pregnant. They were a lovely couple but the lady was extremely anxious which is really understandable. I sent her for extra scans and made her an appointment to see my favourite consultant who was so good with her. He made her feel really comfortable with what was going on.

This lady would ring me on a very regular basis saying the baby was not moving; so I would either visit her at home or she would come to clinic. She was so funny she would ring me and say, its dead again can you bring it back to life. My line was, "I would certainly come and have a listen in," to allay her fears.

By the end of the pregnancy, she would ring and I would say, "Oh, it's dead again is it, and you want me to bring it back to life?"

Bless them they were great, but so anxious. They had made big plans for this baby and would tell me what clothes and baby equipment they had bought. They were so excited.

The lady started having contractions at 36wks and went on to have a normal vaginal birth. The baby cried immediately but was small so was taken to the baby unit to help with its breathing and growing.

I remember visiting her at home when the baby came home and they were so happy. I was quite shocked with the equipment and clothes they had bought.

They lived in a lovely house, had no mortgage and the décor was lovely. Everything they had bought for the baby was second hand, or from a charity shop. You can buy some really lovely things from charity shops these days but it seemed strange to me that having waited so long for a baby, they had bought nothing new at all. That baby was so loved and that was the main thing.

Chapter 31
Breast Cancer in Pregnancy

I had a lady who was diagnosed with breast cancer at 28wks, of pregnancy. She was a lovely lady who already had 4 beautiful children, but this baby was very much wanted. I brought her in to see the consultant who was very supportive and had a conversation with her Oncologist who was reluctant for her to go to full term, as she needed a mastectomy. A compromise was reached and she was decided to deliver her at 36wks. I promised I would be with her if I could.

When the time came for her delivery, she was induced and I went into the delivery ward to deliver her. We had had long conversations before this point about how she would feed her baby, she desperately wanted to breast-feed but this would, of course, delay her having a mastectomy. So, the conversation went to, "Well, can I feed from one breast?"

"Well, yes you could but unfortunately both breasts would fill up with milk." So, this would not help her situation. After a lot of soul searching, she decided that she would give the baby formula and I fully supported her in this. The delivery suite was informed of this and asked not to mention breast feeding; as this just upset her.

This lady was induced at 36weeks and, fortunately, I was around to go in with her. She delivered a beautiful baby girl; but unfortunately, the afterbirth was very reluctant to be delivered. The usual tricks were tried like emptying the bladder, sitting upright on a commode but I was very reluctant to try what normally works—putting the baby on the breast, as this was exactly what we didn't want to do.

After a while, I knew we needed help; so I went out to the desk to inform the senior midwife who knew about the lady's condition and knew that any talk of breast feeding was banned. She came into the room looked at the woman and said put the baby on the breast.

I could have smacked her; the lady burst into tears, the husband was furious and I just said, "That's not going to happen. We need a doctor in here to make a plan."

This lady was taken to theatre and her placenta was delivered and she recovered well. Two weeks after the birth, she was due to have the mastectomy and plans had been made for her to take her baby with her so that they were not separated for a prolonged length of time. She was going to a private hospital so this was not thought to be a problem. I was going on holiday shortly after the birth but promised I would visit her when I returned.

When I returned, from my holiday I kept my promise and visited this lady who had had her mastectomy the week before and was doing well but was obviously still quite emotional. I gave her a hug and asked her how she was feeling; she just burst into tears, bless her. She informed me she had had a visit from the Health Visitor who had asked her how it felt to lose a breast. Not the best question to ask at that point in time. It had obviously been quite difficult for her and she really needed to get used to the idea of her condition. This lady did extremely well; she later on had a reconstruction operation and I saw her not long ago, about 15 years down the line which is fantastic.

I had another lady who had breast cancer which was diagnosed during her pregnancy. She was diagnosed at 32 weeks and delivered at 36 weeks. This lady went on to have a normal delivery and did very well postnatally. I saw her about a year later and she looked so beautiful.

She was still having ongoing treatment and had had a few setbacks. I had a long chat with her. She was with her children, who were so very young. Several months later, I heard that she had relapsed and eventually she died. It was just so sad, she wanted to live so badly. Sometimes, life seems so unfair. Her husband was such a lovely man and took on the role of mum and dad and did a really good job. He had a good support network around him but it must have been so difficult for him and the children. The baby was less than a year old when she died; and she had died on her oldest child's birthday. He was four. These are the times when you feel helpless.

Another lady I looked after was blessed with three children. She lived along with her husband and her parents and they seemed a very close family. When her youngest child was 3 she went out for the night with her friends and apparently took drugs. Unfortunately, she crashed her car and was killed on impact.

I remember hearing about this and thinking, *What a waste, now three young children were without their mother and a young father was left alone to care for them.* This was all due to stupidly taking drugs and then driving. It is so upsetting when you think my other lady who wanted to live so badly and died through no fault of her own. I am sure the lady did not kill herself on purpose, but it's a stark warning, under the influence of anything and getting in a car is pure stupidity.

I had a lovely lady who was expecting her 2nd baby whose husband had been diagnosed with cancer whilst she was pregnant. It was a very difficult situation for her and unfortunately her husband became very ill and unfortunately died whilst she was still pregnant. What a difficult situation to be in, it was so sad. Fortunately, she had a very good support system around her, and I was so surprised at how strong she was. They actually got married in the hospice he had been in.

I managed to be able to go into the hospital to deliver her. She also had a couple of her best friends as her birth partners and they supported her so well. The delivery was a joyous occasion. This lady coped so beautifully when she had taken her baby home. Fortunately, she had a lot of support from her family and her husband's family and friends, but it was so difficult for her.

They say God only gives us pain, which is enough for to cope with; but sometimes I wonder where these women get their strength from. This particular lady was an absolute star, and I do hope she finds happiness for herself and her beautiful children.

One of my favourite people to work with was a health care assistant, Gill. I had looked after her in her pregnancies and had got very fond of her. She was superb at her job very empathetic, extremely clever and picked things up amazingly quickly. She helped me out an awful lot, especially with helping mums' breast feed when I had not got the time to sit with them, also helping out at clinic. The ladies loved her and looked upon her as part of the team. I persuaded her to do her midwifery training and shortly after this she did so.

The course work for her was easy and I tried to help her as much as I could with the practical side. She was a natural and it was quite amusing to see her with patients, it was like listening to me. During her training, we had yet another new manager who thought we should not work together as we were obviously friends. This caused a lot of upset; and I always thought it was a jealousy thing.

Students need to work with different midwives, as this student had, and in different departments to get a rounded view of the profession, but there is no need to cause friction between the midwives. When this girl became a midwife, she felt so bad about the tension, unfortunately she did not stay in the profession, but went off to do a Health Visiting course at which she obviously excelled. She is now working as a Health Visitor and loving it. Shortly after she left, the manager concerned had to re-apply for her job and was not reinstated.

We had frequent changes to our Head of Midwifery; some were very good. One, I only met once in two years. They seemed to take up the position; change things that they thought would work, but often didn't, and held meetings which seems an awful waste of a good midwife.

I know someone has to be in charge but I sometimes felt frustrated at things changing for the sake of change. We had one head of midwifery. She came from a fairly local hospital. A really nice lady but if any new posts came up they were always filled with her colleagues from her former hospital. I began to wonder if there were any midwives left at her last hospital. Shortly after, all these new posts were filled she left and so more changes were made.

Chapter 32
Supervisor of Midwives

During my career as a midwife, I became a Supervisor of Midwives; this meant we supported the midwives in their work life, made sure they were up to date and looked into serious incidents. We met with the midwives at least once a year and had to sign a form, in January each year, to say the midwife was up to date and was competent to practice and work as a midwife. This role took up a lot of time but was very rewarding.

One incident, I remember was a particular midwife, I didn't know her but I met her at the doors of the ward one day when I was leaving. She asked me if I would be her supervisor and I informed her that my list was full but she should speak to one of the managers. I never thought any more about it.

I received a phone call from a manager one day when I was at home asking me if I had signed this midwife's intention to practice form. This was the form we had to fill in by law for every midwife. I told the manager I had not signed it, and it came out that this midwife had forged my signature on the form and told the manager I had told her to do this. Well, to cut a very long story short, this midwife lived in Wales where she had come to the notice of the managers as being incompetent. She worked in England as she was unable to work in Wales. I was very shocked and when shown a copy of the form; my name was not even spelt properly.

In time, this came to a hearing at the Royal Collage of Midwives and I had to attend as a witness. I had never done anything like this before and was quite apprehensive. The hospital was very supportive and allowed one of the other Supervisors to accompany me, as we had to go to Wales for the hearing. The hearing was to last two to three days, I was called as a witness on the second day. It was a very formal hearing and was quite scary. I think they could see how nervous I was as they allowed my Supervisor colleague to sit beside me. Thank goodness for that, my hands were shaking and I held her hand under the desk.

I was asked several questions by the panel then the midwife herself was able to question me. That was an eye opener. She informed me that I had told her to sign the form and that she knew me well. I had worked with her when she was a student. Well either she had a warped memory or I had forgotten her completely, this was not the case I am afraid. She was lying and the panel could see this and she was struck off.

It's a very difficult situation seeing someone go through that but in the end the safety of the mothers and their babies is paramount and that's all that matters.

One cold night, I was called into the hospital as the delivery suite was very busy and a lady who was 28wks into her pregnancy needed transferring to a different hospital, as the special care baby unit was full and would have had difficulty taking the baby after delivery. I duly left my bed and off I went.

When I went into the lady's room I had a chat with her and asked if I could have a look at her before the ambulance was called. She agreed, and when I palpated her abdomen I asked her where the pain was and when she had last had her bowels open. I cannot remember when she told me.

She felt very full in the bowel department. I said to her, "I will ask the consultant if I can rectify this problem before we go in the ambulance, as ambulances are not the most comfortable ride." I duly asked the consultant who, because she was not dilating, agreed for her to have glycerine suppositories. I explained to the lady and she agreed to go ahead.

As she was pre-term, I was reluctant to take her to the bathroom so I took a commode (a mobile toilet) into the room. After administering the suppositories, I left the lady so she could perform in private but gave her the bell and told her I was just outside. Her husband was with her and a few minutes later he opened the door and shouting quick she has had the baby and it is not crying.

Oh flip, I thought, and raced to her room followed by another midwife and a doctor. I looked into the commode and said don't worry it is not the baby. She had had a huge bowel movement; the poor thing looked terrified. "Don't worry, it's fine," I said but I had to make her look before she believed me.

"Oh, I feel so much better she said." I was not surprised.

We transferred this lady to a London hospital and I wondered later how she was doing. A short time after this, I saw the lady when I was in the hospital. She told me she had been discharged the following day and had gone home and had had no problems since. Well that was good to hear but I did think it was a loss of valuable resources.

Chapter 33
Bullying in the Workplace

I have always got on with my colleagues and until this incident happened, I had never been bullied by anyone. For some reason unbeknown to me, a colleague took an intense dislike to me. We worked in a group of 6 midwives who relieved one another when a colleague was off. We would meet in the office each morning and sort out the work for the day. On a regular basis, if we could, we would meet at some point throughout the day to catch up and make sure all the work would be covered.

On a number of occasions, without my knowledge, midwives were meeting but I was not included. I found this out one morning when this midwife asked the group when I was out of the room if they would meet her for a cake and a cup of tea. When I entered the room, a colleague included me in the invitation; when I said yes, the bully then said she could not make it and pulled out.

I just said, "Don't worry, I have enough work to do. I have not the time to meet up," and left the unit. A manager had noticed what was going on and had a conversation with me. I just told her, "It's a problem that's cropped up and it needs sorting as it making my life very uncomfortable." Shortly after this, the midwife was moved to another team and fortunately life got back to normal.

We had a new team leader just after the incident above and she was extremely supportive. She suggested to the team when she had been in post for a while that a member of the team should swop with her for a month to do her job and she would become a community midwife for a month. This idea was not to my liking as I liked to be hands on but I was selected to do it.

It was mind blowing, I hated it. I seemed to go from one meeting to another. I held the hospital bleep on occasions, which was scary. On one of these occasions, when I was holding the bleep, a call came out for all managers to go the main reception where an incident was occurring. I duly went to find a gentleman holding forth with members of the public who were visiting patients in the hospital. He wanted to put the world to right. He thought he had the power to put all the world problems right. He thought that he was Jesus and we should all listen to him.

Flip, my first thought was*, what do you expect me to do, I am a midwife.* I was extremely thankful when other members of the management team arrived and escorted him away. It turned out he had escaped from the local mental health unit, which was situated near the hospital.

I hated my month in the role of a manager and couldn't wait to get back to my proper job as a community midwife. I have great respect for people who feel they can go into management as a midwifery manager but do feel we are losing a great deal of experience to this role.

Chapter 34
Antenatal Classes

At my antenatal classes, I had lots of questions about birth plans. I always answered that, "Birth plans are a great idea, but be flexible, you don't know what you really want until you are in the situation." I had a couple who were very rigid in their wishes. They wanted no pain relief and a very natural birth. I can understand this but know that not all women can achieve this.

This lady started having contractions when I was not on call; but at 1am in the morning the hospital rang me on my land line, asking for my help with this couple. I agreed to go into the hospital, and when I arrived I could hear a lot of shouting coming from one of the rooms. I was asked to go into the room and speak to them as the husband was trying to uphold her wishes and the lady was screaming for pain relief.

I went into the room and asked them what the problem was. It turned out that the lady had told her husband not to let her have any pain relief even if she was asking for it; and if he allowed her to have pain relief she would divorce him. I asked the lady.

"What do you want?"

"Give me pethidine," she said, so I immediately gave her the gas and air whilst I went outside to get some pethidine from the locked cupboard. The husband came out with me and pleaded with me not to give it to her, but I said to him, "I am giving it to her, she needs it, and you can put the blame on me." The poor chap was in a right state but agreed that they could not go like they were.

We went into the room and I gave her the injection, I then reassured her and helped her to breathe during her contractions until the pethidine worked. Some 15 minutes later, she was much more relaxed, and said to me, "Thank God you arrived. I was just about to kill him."

I did say to her, "Your husband was doing as you asked, so you put him in a very difficult position."

I stayed with the lady until she delivered, which was a couple of hours after I arrived. Thank goodness they laughed about what had happened and stayed married. Moral of the story is to be flexible; don't be too regimented in what you want, just go with the flow.

We had a gypsy encampment in our area. I had visited it quite a few times with no problems. On one visit, I was due to weigh the baby; so I had my bag in one hand and my scales in the other. As I went towards the caravan I was visiting, I saw out of the corner of my eye a small terrier dog heading towards me. I knew from the way it was acting, it was going to go for me, but I was helpless to do anything about it.

Well, it bit me on my leg and I was trying to get it off and everyone just disappeared. I managed to do the visit and told them what had happened. They were very apologetic but said it was not their dog. I had to attend the accident an emergency department, and they stitched me up and sent me on my way. I was dreading visiting the site again but, unbeknown to me, the hospital had reported the incident to the police. They told them that they would escort the community midwife for the next visit. I was very grateful but felt a bit silly, having the police escorting me. The dog by this time had been tied on a rope to the caravan which, I must say, relieved me greatly. Thank goodness, that visit was the discharge visit so I did not have to return for a long time

Chapter 35
Problem Pregnancies

I recently had a lovely lady who was having her second baby. She lived on a farm and was about 34wks pregnant. I was doing her antenatal check in my clinic. Her blood pressure was normal; urine was clear. All was well, until I listened in to her baby. The heart beat was very irregular and slow. I checked the lady's pulse to make sure that was not what I was hearing. I listened to the heart rate for a full minute, obviously the lady could hear that something was wrong. I calmly told her, "This is what we are going to do, I am ringing the hospital and you are going to be checked by them as soon as possible." I told her to ring her husband to take her, while I made the phone call to the hospital.

I knew it would be quicker for her husband to take her than to ring an ambulance, also she was booked in for a different maternity unit so I didn't know if the ambulance would take her there. Off she went and I continued with my clinic.

As soon as I had finished, I rang the lady who was at the hospital but had not been seen. She was still sitting in the waiting room. I told her to hand her phone to a member of staff, which she did and I told them, "This lady needs seeing immediately the heart beat was abnormal."

I had a call from the husband a few minutes later to say she had been transferred to the delivery ward as the heart beat was still all over the place. Later that day she was transferred to Oxford for special scans.

The baby appeared to be fine on the scan and she was sent back to the maternity unit. She was kept in for 2 days, by which time the heart beat was back to normal. I saw her weekly after that and sent her back 3 times for the same complaint. Eventually, she delivered at 38 weeks and had a healthy happy baby. No one to this day knows what was happening. I told her that the baby was pole dancing with its cord and having a laugh. Thank goodness, all was well in the end but was very stressful for the lady and her husband. (Also for me.)

Another pregnancy that sticks in my mind is, a lady having her third baby. This lovely lady had two children by her first husband and this one was with a new husband. I booked her for pregnancy and as was my practice sent off a specimen of urine for laboratory testing. The specimen showed that she had a nasty urinary infection; so was given antibiotics. This happened on a fairly constant basis. She needed treatment with antibiotics for each one. I decided that as she had had several urinary infections in early pregnancy; I would refer her to a consultant at the hospital of her choice.

She was seen in the unit and was told it was nothing to worry about. Because of the severity of her infections I asked her to produce a urine specimen very frequently. Unfortunately, each one showed a problem.

At 22wks I heard from the GP that she had been admitted to the hospital to which I was working and was in a medical ward. I went to see her and it was really upsetting. She had sepsis and was extremely ill. She had a really nasty urinary infection, an infected kidney and 2 collapsed lungs. She was extremely poorly.

Thankfully, after several days of treatment and a shunt to her kidney she returned home, but the poor lady really suffered for the rest of her pregnancy. She had several operations on her ureters and in the end, she was delivered at 37wks. Fortunately, the baby was fine but the lady was scheduled for surgery to resolve her problems shortly after the birth.

The district nurses were excellent when all this was happening and were visiting 3 times a day to give intravenous antibiotics, and to dress her wound on a very regular basis. How she coped with her pregnancy and the pain she was in was tremendous.

I visited her weekly in the last 7 weeks of her pregnancy to support her and we became very close. Her husband, her girls and her mother were extremely supportive throughout all her ordeal. When I discharged her from midwifery care, she was still having problems, and was awaiting surgery on her kidneys.

Fortunately, this lady had the supportive family she needed, which made it all a little easier for her.

One lady I had a lot to do with, lived in a village in my area. She had 2 children, a boy and a girl; and was pregnant with her third child. I booked her at home, and then arranged to see her at the surgery. When I saw her for her 15wk appointment, I could not detect a heartbeat. This is always distressing for the woman. I arranged for her to be seen at her hospital of choice.

Unfortunately, the baby had died. It was so upsetting for her and her family. She coped very well but was looking forward to the time when she could hold another baby in her arms. This lady went on to have another pregnancy where exactly the same thing happened again. Poor lady was obviously very upset. I spent a long time talking and comforting her. Eventually, she got pregnant again, and oh my goodness, it was another loss at 15wks. The hospital concerned were very good with her and promised to send off her baby's placenta for histology to find out if there was a problem with that.

Unfortunately, the placenta was not sent off as promised. She was now desperate to have a baby and went to see doctors in London for advice. Soon after doing this, she was pregnant again. She was giving herself blood thinning injections every day, a huge commitment for anyone.

We got to 15wks, and I arranged to see her at home as I felt this was the best plan. Guess what, we had a heartbeat, I don't know who was more relieved, the lady or me. I visited this lady weekly and thankfully she gave birth to a healthy baby. What some women have to go through to get a baby is unbelievable. Women are so strong in their quest for a baby. Her older children were delighted with their new sibling and, thankfully, mum and baby did very well, I was so pleased for them.

One of my favourite stories involves a Vicar's wife. She was a very softly spoken lady who was absolutely charming. She happened to start having contractions when I was on call. She decided she wanted to deliver in the hospital and then go straight home; so I met her on the delivery ward.

She was in a good pattern of contractions and was awaiting the arrival of her husband, who at this point was in Church running a service. He would join us as soon as he could.

The contractions were going well and she was her usual charming self. That was until the contractions got stronger and longer. This is when her husband put in an appearance. He was still wearing his dog collar and was quite surprised to hear his wife in full flow with each contraction.

The language was awful, she was screaming like a banshee. I was trying not to laugh but the poor husband was mortified. Fortunately for all of us she delivered quite soon after her husband arrived and reverted to her normal soft speaking way. I learnt a few new words that night. A few hours later she was discharged home.

I went to visit her the next day wondering what if anything she would say to me. Her husband answered the door, he was apologising about the night before. I assured him it was fine, that I had heard it all before. (well most of it), but I didn't tell him that. The lady herself was back to her softly speaking self. No more was said by any of us about her delivery; but I did wonder what on earth her husband had said to her.

Chapter 36
Triplets

I met a lady who had had triplets and she was at home with them. When I arrived, she was breastfeeding two of the babies and the other one was crying. So, whilst I was talking to her, I fed the crying baby with a bottle for her. She told me her husband wanted her to breastfeed all the babies, but as I told her you were born with 2 nipples and you are doing really well to feed 2 of them. She was breastfeeding different babies with each feed so all babies got breast milk.

I asked her what help she had, she told me her husband was upstairs in his office. I asked again who was helping her, and she started crying. I gave her a hug, and she went on to tell me her husband ran his own business so had to work. He didn't want her parents to help as they would have to stay and he was not happy about that.

My argument was if he wasn't able to help because he was 'Busy' something needed to be sorted or she would not cope. I asked her if she minded me talking to her husband, she told me to go ahead but it would not do any good.

I put the baby back in his cot when he had finished his feed and called the husband down from his office. First of all, I congratulated him on his beautiful babies, and then went into my midwife mode. Your wife needs help she cannot possibly look after 3 babies on her own. If you are unable to provide the help she needs because of your work load, something needed to be sorted before she loses the plot.

He huffed and puffed but eventually agreed that her parents would have to come. I told him this was a really good idea, as they could help with the babies, but also help with the catering for him and his wife and just take the load of his wife's shoulders.

I think he saw the state his wife was in and melted. He told me that he would ring them straight away. I reassured him the babies would not need 3-hour feeds forever and life would get easier. I also told him that a local collage could help, as their students who were taking child courses could come in for a few hours a week to help with the babies.

Fortunately, he was willing for this to happen so I phoned the college from the house and gave the husband the phone so he felt it was his decision. He knew that it would be a huge help for them both. I visited the next day, and lo and behold her parents were there, and were proving to be a great help, because they were retired they were willing to help for as long as they needed it. Phew, that was a relief I had gone home worrying about how this poor lady would cope; thankfully it all turned out beautifully.

Chapter 37
Screening Tests

There is a blood test that ladies can have in early pregnancy to tell them if they are at risk of their babies being born with downs syndrome. Nowadays, ladies can have this done at their 12-week scan and have something called 'nuchal screening' along with a blood test to assess their risk. Ladies are told about the tests and have the option of having or not having them.

Many years ago, before nuchal screening came in I had a lady who I explained the blood test to. She and her husband decided not to have the test. They had two other children and were happy just to enjoy the pregnancy and have whichever baby they were given.

This lady's pregnancy went well and eventually she gave birth to a beautiful baby girl. Unfortunately, the baby had Downs Syndrome. Whilst she was in the hospital she was seen by paediatricians and midwives who all asked her why she did not have the blood test, and why her midwife had not told her about it.

She assured them; she had been told and that although her baby had the syndrome, it was their baby and she would be loved. I have always believed that none of us are given anything that we cannot cope with and for some reason parents who could care for these babies were sent them. They were a very loving couple and coped beautiful with their baby. I saw them often about with her and they were so proud. The moral of this tale is not everyone wants to know if their baby is destined to have a problem. We should respect their wishes and support them in their decisions.

Weekend Clinics

The weekend clinic, oh, what a joy that was. Our managers in their wisdom thought it would be a good idea to run a post-natal clinic on the weekends so that the ladies and their families could visit us instead of us visiting them.

When it first started it was a nightmare, there were no appointments and you could sit for ages then everyone would turn up together. It was not my favourite place and, thankfully, I was out on visits most of the time and that was fine by me.

Thank goodness, I worked in a rural area so the other midwives were more than happy for me to do these visits. Once the clinic became established, an appointment system was introduced and it became much better. One weekend clinic I remember well was an absolute nightmare. I had agreed to cover that weekend clinic after I had retired.

Appointments were every 15mins with an hour break for lunch. There was another midwife, myself and a maternity assistant running the clinic and it was busy. I seemed to be seeing patient after patient and did not see my colleagues at all.

At 12:30 I went to the desk wondering what was going on as the waiting room was heaving. The other midwife was now where to be seen so I just had to get on with it. After seeing the next lady, I saw the maternity assistant who told me the other midwife had gone off for her lunch! I was not really amused but carried on regardless.

As we saw patients, we signed off each one on the register, to make sure no woman was left waiting too long. At one point during the morning a husband pointed out to me that a man was hanging out of a window in the opposite building. I looked up and thought, *Well that's all I need, a jumper*. It turned out that the gentleman had been somehow locked into a room in the general clinic and was trying everything to notify someone. Thank goodness, a timely phone call did the trick.

The clinic was supposed to finish at 4pm but was still going at 5pm. I was exhausted; had nothing to eat and only had a small glass of water all day. I was down for the clinic the next day as well so was more than fed up. By the time the clinic finished and I got home, it was 6pm.

On the Sunday, I arrived in the office to ask who was down for doing clinic with me. Thankfully, it was a different midwife from the day before. I was dreading the day as thought it would be the same as the day before, but it was a breeze. We took patients in rotation, made each other drinks and the clinic ran smoothly.

The other midwife asked me what had gone on the day before as she was looking at the clinic list. It turned out I had seen 17 patients and the other midwife had seen 4 and the maternity assistant had seen 5. Not a fair share out of the work but now I knew why it had been such a busy clinic. Apparently, the other midwife had taken a two-hour lunch break, and the maternity assistant that had been on duty was known for being extremely slow. What a difference a day makes, this clinic was great, it ran very well and finished on time. Working together as a team works wonders.

Chapter 38
Complaints

I to the most part have had a really good career with no problems with complaints until the last year I was working as a midwife. First bookings were at the time being done in the lady's own home. One lady, I contacted about her appointment asked me if I would mind booking her at her mother's house in Newport Pagnell as their house was being renovated.

This was not a problem so we booked her there, and I arranged to see her at the clinic when she was 15wks pregnant. When I arrived at the clinic the following Tuesday there was a message asking me about her scan date, and could I let her know about it.

The GP usually sent this form off so I checked on the computer and the form had not been sent. I sent off the form and tried to contact this lady to tell her, but the mobile number she had given me was unobtainable. I used the landline number she had given me and left a message for her. I thought no more about it. The next day, I was on duty I had a very rude message from the lady's husband telling me I had ruined their lives, and how dare I leave a message on her parent's phone as they didn't know she was pregnant. I was shocked; so, tried to ring him but had to leave a message as he was unavailable.

I went into the surgery and found out that he had also reported me to the Practice Manager who had been verbally abused by him. I checked on the computer and the number I had been given as theirs at the booking was the one on the screen. I spoke to the husband that lunch time he was very unhappy that I had left a message and said I should have known the number was his wife's mother's house.

I was very upset at all this, but as I tried to explain to him I did not have a crystal ball and was using the information they had given me. Well, he still thought I had ruined their lives and obviously wanted to tell their parents themselves. I totally understood this but I don't know how I could have acted differently. I told him that I would arrange for another midwife to look after them and he agreed this was a good idea. The Practice Manager was extremely supportive, she realised that they were telling lies about where they lived so that they could stay as patients at the surgery.

I asked her not to strike them off the books just yet as I thought the couple would think it was me who had instigated it. I rang my manager who was very supportive. I told her what had happened and she just told me to forget it, she had never had a complaint about me before and was not going to act on this. I should phone the midwife who worked nearby and ask her to take over her care.

I rang the midwife who was extremely shocked. She had never seen me so upset but bless her she agreed to take over her care. I had never ever had a day like this and hoped I never have one again. I went home at the end of the day completely drained and exhausted.

I feel so lucky that I have such a lovely group of ladies who when they heard about what had happened, were so supportive and couldn't believe what had happened. They did not hear about this from me but I work in a small community and things get around. Apparently, the lady concerned had told her pregnant friends about this awful midwife. They had stuck up for me and told her she was losing out on a lovely midwife. I am so lucky to work in the area that I do with supportive colleagues and patients.

Chapter 39
More Home Births

One very cold night, I was called to a home birth in a place called New Bradwell. When I arrived at the house it was a youngish woman obviously in labour; but on her own in the house with two small children. I introduced myself and she told me she had recently moved from London as her husband had left her, and that's why she wanted a home birth.

I asked her who was to look after her when she had the baby and who would look after the other children if they woke up before she delivered. Poor girl had no relatives in the area but I told her that even if she delivered at home, I was very reluctant to leave her at home on her own, with 3 children to care for. She seemed to think the job of the 2nd midwife was to look after the other children. When I explained this was not the case she became a little upset; but said she had made a friend of a lady who lived locally.

I told her to go with the flow and when the time came for her to deliver we would ring her friend and ask her to attend to look after the children until her mother could come from London. During the course of the chat about her labour wishes, she told me that she would need an episiotomy (a cut to help make more room for the baby), and I discussed this with her and said if it was needed that would be done, but I explained that if she listened to me and delivered the baby slowly it may not be necessary. She was very sceptical but I just said wait and see what happens.

The labour continued and the time came for me to call the 2nd midwife. The midwife arrived and the children were now awake so we called her friend and, fortunately, she came quite quickly. The time came for her to push. I just told her do what her body telling you to do. When the head is visible we will breathe the baby out. This lady was great she did exactly as I asked and delivered her baby with no episiotomy necessary. She told me that I was the first midwife who had talked her through the birth as I did and was ecstatic that she didn't need sutures.

It just shows that if we can gain the woman's trust the delivery can be so rewarding. The lady's friend was able to stay with her until her mother arrived, so we left a very happy lady and healthy baby.

I attended a birth one night for a great couple, who were so in love. This was their first baby and they were so excited. When I arrived, the lady was in a really good pattern of labour and was coping very well. They decided they wanted to have as normal a birth as possible and were really supportive to one another. The husband was great and was so in tune with his wife it was lovely to see.

The night went well and it became time to call the 2nd midwife. Just before she arrived, the lady stated that she wanted to push. I advised her to do what her body was telling her to do. Every time she pushed, the husband pushed and kept farting. It was so funny. I have very rarely seen a lady who could not push for laughing. We were all laughing when the 2nd midwife arrived. She came into the room and must have wondered what was going on. She had not been there very long when she too was laughing. The baby was delivered to a room full of laughter. The husband was very apologetic, but we told him he should take up a doulas job so more women could laugh through their deliveries.

Episiotomies

Talking about episiotomies. I had a student with me who was in her third year of training; and she had done all she needed to do, enough deliveries; all her assignments were in and passed and everything was on line for her passing her exams; except that she had never done an episiotomy. She had been told that she could not pass her final exams without doing one. I was shocked, I had not done one for 20 years, and I certainly was not going to let the student do one just so that she call pass her exams.

I spoke to the tutors, and we discussed the issue. It was part of the course that all students had to do an episiotomy in their training; but, as I pointed out to her, we could not do one just so that she could pass her exams. Fortunately, the tutor agreed with me and arranged to talk to her colleagues about this issue. The outcome of this was that students could now pass their exams without doing an episiotomy and that this would be looked at in the first year after they became qualified midwives and were working on the delivery ward. This was a good idea as midwives in community saw all the normal births where episiotomy was usually unnecessary, but in the hospital situation where ladies with problems were seen it was more likely that they would be able to fulfil this commitment.

Cheeky Patients

One night, I was called into the unit to help as they were busy. I was asked to look after a lady who was in good labour and had her husband and her 3-year-old child with her. I entered the room and during conversation, they told me that they were American and that they were here to have their baby.

I asked if they now lived here, they responded that, "Oh no; but, it is cheaper to get a flight to Britain to have the baby than to have the baby at home." I was astonished and not best pleased but the delivery was fairly imminent so I just did my job. I was concerned that the 3-year-old was in the room, he was quite boisterous and I asked if he was going to be there at the delivery, the answer was well he will have to as we have nobody to look after him. The lady was making quite a lot of noise and the child was obviously upset but it was a difficult situation.

At one point, I went to the desk and asked if there was a maternity assistant who could look after the child during the actual delivery. This is not their job but, thankfully, one of these ladies came into the room specifically to make sure the child was all right. The parents didn't seem to mind if the child was there or not but we gave them the opportunity for the child to leave the room; they decided not to take it. The lady delivered shortly afterwards, but I can still see the look of horror on the child's face. Once the lady had delivered the placenta and was cuddling her baby, I went out to my colleagues and asked them to let the overseas officer know in the morning. I don't know the outcome of this but I do hope they got a bill for the hospital's services. I know that if a British woman went to an American hospital they would be asked for their credit card before they were given treatment.

It is always lovely to deliver your own ladies; and I worked in an area that had a high home birth rate. One of my ladies was due to have her third baby and had decided to have a home birth; so, we booked her and the day came for her to deliver. I had a 3rd year student Gill with me and off we went to her house. Everything was calm and peaceful and she was doing very well.

She had decided to deliver in a pool, so we got the pool filled up, and when it was at the right temperature she got in and found it to be very beneficial for her pain relief. She was calm and she progressed quite quickly. We all sat waiting patiently for her to want to push and eventually the time came and she delivered a beautiful baby who looked perfect but big.

She cuddled her baby and eventually we got her out of the pool and weighed her baby. I don't know who was most surprised, the baby weighed 11lbs 7ozs. Gosh, normal delivery, no stiches, the student Gill was extremely proud of herself as she should have been. It is quite rare for a baby of that size to be delivered without any problems, but this was just a routine delivery for the very happy lady and her beautiful big boy.

Another home birth in the pool called me out with my student Gill. All was going well and the lady was progressing very well and baby's heartbeat was normal throughout. The 2nd midwife was called and the lady duly delivered.

Unfortunately, the baby failed to breathe spontaneously, so I took the baby from the mother who was still in the pool and asked the 2nd midwife to ring for an ambulance; also to ring the surgery for a GP as we were 2 mins away from the surgery.

Fortunately, the resuscitation worked and we got the baby to breathe within a short time. Talk about the cavalry arriving, within minutes, a paramedic arrived, the GP and 2 practice nurses attended. The room was full and I was extremely grateful to them all for acting so quickly. The baby went on to breathe normally and the crisis was averted. We did transfer them into the Unit so that the baby could be seen by the neonatal staff but, fortunately, did very well and came home two days later. That's a delivery you do not forget.

One of my ladies was extremely excited to be having her 5th baby but was desperate for a girl as she had 4 boys. I had the discussion with her that it was more likely for her to have another boy, as this seemed to follow a pattern, but she wouldn't hear anything negative about the sex of her baby.

She decided not to find out the sex at her scan but told me she had bought all pink things and a pink lined baby basket. I was slightly worried about her as I wondered what would happen if the baby was a boy. The pregnancy went well and she eventually delivered a baby boy.

I was really worried for her sanity and quite apprehensive when I went to visit her. Fortunately, she was well and totally in love with her baby. It turned out she had had a difficult delivery with the baby going into distress and having to go into the special care baby unit. I listened to her story, thankfully, all had turned out well but the lady realised she was lucky her baby was well and take home with her. I was really relieved and pleased that she was so smitten with her baby and he went on to be a very welcome member of their family.

I used to do my own antenatal classes for my own women in the evenings in the surgery when it was closed. We had some great times, and it's a way of getting to know your patients very well. Most of the husbands/partners came too and it was good to get to know them better.

We had some interesting times and I tried to make them fun. My way was; *down to earth, tell it as it is and to answer any questions truthfully.* Some of the questions were funny like: "Where is the nearest pub?" "What if I poo?"

My answer to the poo question was midwives get excited when people poo when they are pushing, as we know they are pushing in the right way.

My use of the surgery was really useful as I lived only about four miles away. When the class had finished I had to shut the surgery and set the alarm.

On one occasion, I had my great maternity assistant with me. We turned off all the lights, made sure all the doors were shut and Gill stood at the back of the surgery ready for me to run to the back door to leave the premises. We did this and left via the back door. Turned the corner and the 6ft gate was padlocked. We had no key to it so we wondered what we were going to do.

We couldn't go back into the surgery as I didn't know if the code to get out was the same as to go in, so we were laughing saying who is going to climb the gate. Gill was volunteered and set about climbing the gate. I was no help as I was laughing hysterically. She got to the top of the gate and then suddenly the gate flew open and she was left swinging. We then had to get her down. That was more difficult than getting her up, but in the end, we managed it. We laughed all the way home about this. I just wish I had had my mobile with me so I could have videoed it. After this incident I always went out of the main entrance to avoid it happening again.

Chapter 40
Winding Down

The time had come for me to wind down and start thinking about retirement. I was well over 60, working 4 days a week and running a busy surgery. I decided to cut down my hours and see how it went, so I cut down to 3 days a week. This was much better for me as I looked after Evee one day a week and then I had a free day, so I was able to carry on for a number of years.

I still remember well when Charlotte went back to her job as a teacher. Evee was 6 months old and totally breast-fed. Charlotte and Justin had tried her on the bottle several times as she had wanted to carry on breast feeding at night and daytime when she could but, obviously, Evee would have to be fed when this was not available. Charlotte dropped her off and left sobbing; it was awful to see, but I promised her she would be fine and I would do my best to get milk into her.

Well, she was fine for a few hours and then the time came to feed her. I tried the bottle but she was not sucking it, so I used one of my tricks, I put milk into a 10 ml syringe, put the bottle in her mouth and squirted small amounts of milk into her mouth whilst the teat was in her mouth. I managed to get about 2 ounces into her. Then had a lovely cuddle but knew it would not keep her going for long. The next feed arrived and I did the same and she started sucking the teat.

The funniest part of the day was when Charlotte burst into the house to fetch her gorgeous baby. I gave Evee to her and Evee grabbed her jumper, pulled it down and latched onto the breast, Charlottes face was priceless, and believe it or not Evee took a bottle when necessary after that.

One lady who wanted a home birth lived in a beautiful house, very neat and tidy and carpeted throughout the lounge in a deep white shag pile carpet. She wanted a water birth and we were happy with this as she had no risk factors but a bit worried about the carpet.

When the time came for her delivery the floors were completely covered in plastic which was great and she laboured very well and eventually delivered a beautiful baby. We advised her to get out of the pool to deliver the afterbirth but she decided she wanted to stand up to deliver it. She was quite a tall lady about 5ft 11in and when she felt the placenta was coming she stood up.

I was 2nd midwife at this birth so I took the baby whilst the other midwife was ready to catch the placenta. Unfortunately, she was looking elsewhere when the placenta was eventually delivered, it splashed into the pool and we were really shocked to see there was mess all over the curtains and walls. Oops. The mother was not happy, but we did ask her to get out of the pool to deliver the afterbirth.

The husband was great and told us it was an accident and not our fault. We did feel bad though. I went to see the lady the next day and the decorators were in. The curtains had been sent to the cleaners and peace was restored. I apologised about the mess, but they were so happy with how the delivery went and with their baby, that they were really nice about it and even bought us a bouquet of flowers.

One New Year's Day, I was in Olney doing my visits when I got a phone call from one of my ladies who thought she had gone into labour three weeks before her due date.

I made my way to her house, and she was definitely in labour. The lady was a type 1 diabetic, so it was important that she got into the hospital as soon as possible for a safe delivery. I rang the ambulance who informed me there would be a thirty-minute delay due to a road accident. The ambulance would have to be diverted from Bedford. This was the lady's third delivery so we had not got the time to wait. I told the husband to put the children in his car and make his way to the hospital. I took the decision to put the lady in my car and take her to the delivery ward. This is not supposed to happen, we are not allowed to take patients in our car but I could not see I could do anything else. I quickly rang the Delivery Suite and asked them to be ready for this lady. As it was a Bank Holiday, the roads were fairly clear so I put on my hazard lights and hoped we would make it to the hospital without the police stopping me for speeding.

We arrived on the delivery ward and were quickly sent into a room. The husband followed us and within five minutes the baby was born so, fortunately, she was in the right place for a safe delivery. The baby was quite quickly admitted to the special care baby unit so that its blood sugars could be regulated. The lady did very well and she and her baby were home within five days. Nobody said a word to me about taking the lady in my car. I think I did the right thing but hope I don't have to do it again.

I passed an exam to be able to examine babies for their neonatal (first baby) check. It was really useful, as it helped the doctors out and it was very satisfying for me.

The lady above who had delivered at home was one of the babies I checked. The baby was absolutely fine. I always talked the parents through what I was doing so that they understood. When I had finished checking the baby, the husband made a comment; that his baby had bigger testicles than his three-year-old. I told him that they always looked bigger at birth, but they usually equal themselves out. He asked me if I would mind having a look at his three-year-old's testicles; I explained to them, I was happy to look but was not trained in checking older children.

It turned out the young boy's testicles were not where they should be and I could see the scrotum was extremely small. I advised them to take him to see the GP so that they could examine the child. It turned out he had undescended testicles and needed an operation. It is something that is usually picked up much earlier than three so I was quite surprised. The little boy had an operation to put the problem right and all was well. It is better for boys to have this operation before they are one but as it was not picked up this had not happened.

One of my ladies who lived in the same village as I, had a baby that I was asked to examine, she was a lovely looking baby, healthy and pink and feeding well, so I had no worries before I examined her. When I listened in to her heart I could hear that the heartbeat was abnormal. I ascertained that the baby had a heart murmur. I explained this to the parents and let them listen to the baby's heart. I then rang the GP who promised to visit later that morning. I tried to reassure the parents but obviously this was very worrying for them. The GP visited and referred the baby to the hospital. The baby had a heart scan and was found to have a small hole in the ventricle of the heart. Fortunately, this was very likely to close on its own within a few weeks. Thankfully, this happened and the baby did very well. I see her often going down the road with her mum or dad to catch the bus for school. I found this more stressful because I knew the parents but, thankfully, all turned out well.

I remember booking a lady for pregnancy at another surgery she was having her first baby and we went through her medical history and then came on to her next of kin etc. I asked her who the baby's father was and she gave me his name and date of birth. Then I asked her about his occupation. Well she said he is an armed robber. Ok, well that's a first. It turned out he was in prison at the time and would not be released until after the baby was born. I discussed with the girl about his occupation and we decided between us to leave it blank. I did feel sorry for her as she had to go through the pregnancy alone. Her parents were not in her life so I arranged for her to be seen by the teenage pregnancy midwife. Although, she was just over the age for that particular midwife, she would get the support she needed. This was done and the pregnancy progressed well very well. She got all the support she needed and did extremely well.

Chapter 41
Managers!!!

The nights on call were becoming quite difficult so I decided to cut down on my hours again and I began to work Tuesday Fridays and one weekend a month. This meant that I only did 1 on-call a month or two at the most which was so much better. I still got my fair share of deliveries, usually at the weekend as I could be on call Friday or Saturday. I still had the same number of women to look after but, somehow, I managed it. It just meant that I couldn't help other midwives as much as I had done in the past.

Weekends were always more relaxed. We had the same number of visits to do but no clinics in community and no managers. It was also easy to get into the car park. It just shows how many managers, administrative staff etcetera who didn't work weekends as the car park was almost empty. We all helped one another at the weekends much more than we were able to in the week and we all worked well together.

I remember one Saturday I was out on the community and it was snowing. The weather was getting worse throughout the day and at 4pm I had a phone call from a manager who was calling from her home to tell me that some staff could not get into the hospital because of the weather and community girls were being called in.

It beggars belief that she thought we could get in when others couldn't, but I did eventually make it to the hospital and was there most of the night. Ambulances were bringing the women in as they couldn't drive in and I must admit I thought I would be stranded at there for an eternity. Miraculously, at about 4am it started to rain and the weather cleared. I went home about 6am totally exhausted and ready to meet my bed.

I had a call at 12 midday saying community was extremely short as four of us had been in the hospital overnight. My reply was, "I am not fit to work please send the hospital ward staff out to help." It was not received very well, but it is a midwife's duty to say if she is too tired to work as that's when mistakes can happen.

When I went into the office on the Tuesday, the manager concerned came towards me and I thought, *Flip, I am in for a mouthful,* but she said, "Thank you for helping out at the weekend."

She left the room and my colleagues looked at me and said, "Good for you for telling them that you felt unable to help."

It does sometimes feel that community girls help out in the hospital but this was very rarely the other way around. Sometimes you just have to stand up for yourself.

The same manager who had called us all in to the unit because of the snow started calling us in on a regular basis in the early evening usually about 6 or 7pm. With time, this was getting a bit annoying. We found out we were being called in to relieve the hospital ward midwives so that they could have a meal break. This was shocking to us as we had been working all day and were lucky if we had a meal break.

I am pleased to say that after discussions with our community manager this was deemed unfair. We were always happy to help out in an emergency, but this was just taking the biscuit. It was stopped soon after this, thank goodness; obviously our hospital colleagues deserve a meal break but not to the detriment of the community staff.

One morning when I went into the hospital I went to see a lady of mine who I had sent in on the previous day, as her C-section scar was very infected and leaking. Whilst I was talking to her, the consultant arrived, he was a good doctor but his bedside skills were somewhat lacking. He arrived at the bedside pulled down the covers without speaking to the lady. I quickly pulled the curtains around her as he said well I know what we need to do here. Before I could breathe, he pulled a pair of scissors out of his pocket and poked them into the woman's scar; the result was fluid poured out of her and she was extremely shocked as I was. I cleaned her up and dressed her wound and went to talk to the Sister in charge of the ward.

She was shocked when I told her what had happened and immediately went to the lady's bedside to talk to her. I must admit, the wound swelling had gone down an awful lot; but I dread to think what bugs those scissors had on them. This lady was taken to theatre later that day, she had her wound cleaned and redressed and, fortunately, it healed up well, although she was on antibiotics for 10 days. Thankfully, she came to no harm despite what had been done to her. I was elated when I heard later that the consultant was due to retire. I do know that the lead consultant was advised as to what had happened and hopefully he never did that again.

Chapter 42
Maternity Emergencies

One birth I shall never forget was for a lady who wanted a home birth for her 3rd baby. She rang me one morning when I was in the office and told me her waters had gone and that they were brown. This meant that the baby had had a poo in the bag of waters and was not conducive to a home birth. I told her I was in the hospital and she should make her way to the hospital and I would meet her there.

I duly did this and the husband was duly sent home to get her notes as we needed these for all her history and details of the pregnancy. I proceeded to examine the lady and then asked her if she would mind me performing a vaginal examination to see if she had made any progress. The lady agreed to this and I proceeded to assess her progress. I was in the room alone with the lady and on examination found that she had a cord prolapse, this meant that the cord was in front of the baby's head and is a medical emergency. It is the midwives job to keep the oncoming head away from the cord, so that it is not compressed; as this would cause death to the baby.

I informed the lady what was happening and told her I was going to call for help and as we were alone in the room. I needed her to move onto all fours and stick her bottom in the air with my hand inside her to stop anything happening to the baby. I also had to shout for help as I could not reach the bell to summon help.

Fortunately, I was in a room near the midwife's station; so, help soon came. This lady was taken to theatre with my hand still inside her and given a general anaesthetic to deliver the baby by C-section as a vaginal delivery was not safe for the baby. This poor lady had had two vaginal births so obviously was very upset; also could not wait for her husband to arrive, as it was an emergency. The delivery went ahead and my hand stayed inside her until the baby had been delivered. This is really difficult as I couldn't remove my fingers. I was not scrubbed for theatre and eventually was able to remove them. It took me a while to get feeling back into my hand, but I had to go and greet the husband and tell him what had happened. The baby was born well and cried immediately it was a big relief to everyone. The lady was quite traumatised by what had happened and needed several visits to explain what and why things had happened as they did. I recently met this lady in a shop when I was out with my daughter and she greeted me saying I bet you have not forgotten me. My answer to that was, "No, and I never will." Her little boy had grown up very well and met all his mile stones. It was a great outcome and very pleasing for all concerned.

I looked after a lady who was having her second baby, her first child a son had been born at 28wks, no one knew why this had happened, but for this birth she wanted to have a home birth. I discussed this with her and told her if she went to 37wks that this would be possible. Her son had been in the neonatal intensive care unit for many weeks and, although small and wearing glasses, he was absolutely fine. This lady's pregnancy went very well and she eventually went into labour at 41wks, it was a lovely delivery and she was so happy to be able to breast-feed her daughter and cuddle her straight away. Her son was a very happy proud big brother, and it was great to see them as a happy family.

A lady I looked after, lived in a village just outside my area. She was a lovely lady who had lost her first baby to a stillbirth. In this pregnancy she was expecting twins and was obviously quite anxious. I saw her regularly at the surgery and got to know her and her husband very well. Eventually the twins were delivered. She had two girls and she returned home with them very quickly and was doing very well.

When I visited, they insisted that I had a cup of tea and this was duly drunk with a grimace. I don't know what they did to their tea but it was quite difficult to drink. On one of my visits, I had a student with me and I warned her about the 'tea' and off we went. The lady and her husband were delightful and were so happy with their babies, who were both doing very well. Then came the tea, we duly drank it and when we got out to the car the student said well I know why it tasted so awful. I must have looked surprised so she asked me if I had not seen all the tins of carnation milk stacked up in the lounge. I had not seen them but now I understood. Bless them, they didn't use ordinary milk for their guests as they thought carnation milk made a better cup of tea. I beg to differ but it was very sweet of them. This lady sends me a Christmas card every year, and the twins are now young teenagers. They were what I called 'the salt of the earth'; very happy. They had little money but the children were delightful.

Chapter 43
Pre-Eclampsia

Pre-eclampsia is a disease that is dangerous in pregnancy, the symptoms can include high blood pressure, protein in urine and swelling of limbs and face. Patients can get headaches and flashing lights in front of the eyes. It can make women really ill and most of the time they don't know they are ill.

I remember two patients especially who were really ill with this disease. I was doing my rounds one morning in Newport Pagnell when I had a phone call from a lady telling me she felt very unwell and her head was pounding. I was just around the corner from her so I went to visit her. Her blood pressure was very high she had a lot of protein in her urine and was very swollen. Her husband was at work so I called an ambulance and sent her into hospital; I heard later that she had started fitting when she reached the Delivery Suite and was taken to the operating theatre for an emergency C-section. Delivery is the cure for pre-eclampsia but sometimes it can turn into something called 'Help Syndrome.' This magnifies in kidney and blood clotting problems and can be very dangerous for the mother. This lady was taken to Intensive care and was looked after on a one to one basis for 3 days, until she was well enough to go to the post-natal ward. Her baby had been born at 36 weeks but was doing very well on the baby unit, and she was able to be reunited with her. It was shocking to hear how ill this lady had been. I saw her on the intensive care unit and she was so happy that she had rung me. She was just going to go to bed and try and get rid of her headache; I am so pleased she rang me, as she would have been alone in the house until her husband had returned from work, some 6 hours after I had seen her. It was a happy result all round, and mum and baby did very well with no repercussions of the illness on either of them.

Another lady I remember with this disease, was a lady who attended the antenatal clinic I was running in my surgery. She was 34 weeks pregnant and as soon as she walked into the room, I knew she was in trouble. Her face was extremely swollen, and she had on dark glasses to shade her eyes from the light. Fortunately, her husband was with her and after I had taken her blood pressure which was very high and tested her urine which was full of protein I rang the maternity unit and asked them to see her. This was her first pregnancy so, obviously, it was very frightening for them. I tried to reassure them but I told them you will probably be admitted for observation, and the worst thing that could happen is that you have to deliver your baby to resolve the problem.

This lady was admitted to the delivery ward where she was observed closely for 24 hours. When her blood test showed that things were getting worse, she was taken to theatre and had an emergency C-section. The baby was small, at 3lbs 4ozs, as they sometimes are with this problem; but did very well. Fortunately, after the delivery the lady's blood pressure started to go down and she got well quite quickly. The lady and her husband wanted to know how I knew by looking at her that she had a problem. I explained to them that as I knew her very well I knew what she usually looked like and was aware of the swelling immediately.

The husband was upset that he had not noticed that she was swollen. I explained to him, he saw her all the time and usually it is difficult to see the changes that are happening. I had not seen her for 2 weeks so I noticed the difference. The moral of this tale is it is so important to know your ladies. To have a case loading midwife is a good way of keeping ladies safe. The baby came home after being in the unit for 1 month and did very well.

The lady above was obviously quite worried about what would happen if she had another baby. I explained to them that it was unlikely to happen again although not unheard of. I also told her that if she kept her husband and didn't exchange him for someone else she was less likely to have a problem in her next pregnancy. This lady went on to have a very normal pregnancy some 2 years later.

Chapter 44
Supporting Your Patients

Late one evening I had a phone call from a colleague, she had had a phone call about one of my ladies who had delivered at another unit. The lady had been very upset by comments made to her about her baby. She was told by one midwife that her baby had 'squinty eyes and looked weird'. No one wants to be told this, and the lady and her husband were obviously very upset. Another midwife had seen her baby and told her she thought her baby had the appearance of a downs syndrome baby; then left the room.

Obviously, they were extremely upset, and had discharged themselves from the unit. I rang her and found she was already at home and could hear how upset she was so I offered to visit. This was accepted and off I went; by this time it was midnight.

When I arrived at the house, I gave the lady a hug, accepted a cup of tea and sat down to discuss the situation with them. The baby was in its cot, I looked at her and then at the husband and said, "Well I think the baby looks just like her dad," they then asked me to examine her. She had none of the signs of downs syndrome. Her eyes were level, her hands had the normal markings. There was not a gap between the big toe and the next toe and its heart also sounded normal. I asked them if they had any photographs of the husband when he was a baby and was duly given one. The baby was an exact replica of the dad. I told them I couldn't give them a written guarantee that their baby was not a downs baby; but I was happy in my own mind that she was perfectly normal. I assured them I would speak to the GP the next day and would ask him to visit.

The end of this tale; The baby was normal, all the stress and upset had been unnecessary. I do think all professionals need to be careful with their words, to think before they say what they were feeling, without having all the information needed to make a decision. Thankfully all turned out well and the couple were able to enjoy their beautiful baby daughter.

Breech Babies

I was on annual leave at home when I received a phone call from one of my ladies. She had my home number as we had the same cleaner and she was pregnant with her 4th baby. This lovely lady had had 3 vaginal births but this 4th baby was in the breech position. She had been advised by a colleague that she could have the baby turned into the right position and wanted my advice. I said to her well you could do that or you could deliver the baby vaginally; but I did wonder why this baby was in the breech position.

We discussed her options and I knew that she had private medical care so I said why don't you treat yourself and have the baby at the Portland Hospital, delivered by my friendly consultant. I told her to discuss her options with her husband and asked her to make an appointment at the surgery for the next week when I was back to discuss it further.

When I saw her at clinic with her husband she told me she wanted to deliver the baby by C-section. I told her she could do this at the local hospital but she had decided she wanted to go to the Portland. I rang the consultant and he arranged to see her in his private consulting rooms. The outcome of this delivery was that the baby was born safely by my friendly consultant; and the baby had what is called a true knot in the cord. This means that if the baby had been turned the knot could have been pulled tight and the baby could have died. Thank goodness, all turned out well, and she and her husband were extremely happy with the outcome; and she really enjoyed her experience.

When I was in clinic one day I examined a lady, who was having her first baby and thought that her baby was in the breech position, so I made an appointment for her at the antenatal day assessment unit for the next day as she was already 37wks. I asked her to ring me when she had been. I got the call and she told me she had been examined and reassured that the baby was in the head down position. It is sometimes difficult to diagnose a breech baby with a first-time mum as their muscles are quite tight, so I was happy that she could have a normal vaginal birth. Two weeks later, this lady went in to deliver her baby.

Guess what, the baby was in the breech position; and she had to have an emergency C-section. I saw her in the hospital and it turned out from her notes that she had been seen by a student midwife whose mentor had not checked after her examination. I was a bit taken aback and talked to the sister in charge of the day assessment unit. I knew this was not normal practice and after this discussion new protocols were brought in so that if a baby was thought to be breech the woman should be scanned. All turned out well for this lady and her baby, but it would have been better for all if she had known that her baby was upside down so that the delivery was less stressful for her and her husband.

Poorly Babies

On one of my normal post-natal visits I visited a lady who had had her first baby. The baby was 5 days old and had been delivered normally. As soon as I saw the baby, I knew she was in trouble. She was pale and floppy and had a low temperature. The mother told me she had not fed very well and that her poos were very loose and a pale colour. I examined the baby and her nappy and found that her poo was almost white, which is obviously not normal. I told the lady I was worried about the baby and was going to call the GP for advice.

I rang the surgery and talked to the GP who was on call and she asked me if the baby needed to be seen urgently. I was trying to be laid back for the sake of the parents and I replied, "Yes, she needs to be seen now." The GP was great, she knew that I did not ask for help unless I was really worried, she arrived within 5 minutes.

The outcome was that the baby was sent into the local hospital and after tests was transferred to Kings Collage Hospital in London, where it was found that the baby had galactosemia and was intolerant to lactose. This meant that the baby was unable to absorb its feeds and so had become extremely ill. The baby was in the London hospital for several weeks and, thankfully, did very well. The baby was put on special milk. The mother's breast milk was not tolerated by the baby. Although, it was an awful shock for the parents they were absolutely wonderful with coping with the baby. Two years later, the lady had another baby which was tested just after it was born for the intolerance and guess what; that baby also had the same intolerance. These children did very well as they got older but it was quite difficult for the parents.

One very cold snowy night, I had a phone call from my manager. She informed me that a lady of mine had gone into labour and was booked for a home birth was refusing to go into the hospital to deliver. She asked me if I would mind going. I was not on call but, thankfully, my husband was home to care for the children so I agreed to go. I told my manager I have no equipment but was informed she would get another midwife to bring the equipment out to me.

When I arrived at the house the lady was in a good pattern with her contractions and was coping very well. Thankfully, she did not need any pain relief as I had not got any at that point. The labour continued she got to 8cm and no sign of the second midwife with the equipment.

I phoned the hospital and they told me she was on her way. I reassured the lady and told her to do what her body was telling her to do. After a short interval she wanted to push so I prepared for delivery as best I could. As the head delivered the midwife arrived, which was a comfort, fortunately, all was well and the baby was delivered safely.

When I went into the office the next morning, I was told that the manager had been first on call but she was having her hair done.!!! The first thing I did that day was to put a delivery pack and an instrument pack into the boot of my car so I was prepared if that ever happened again. I was told by my colleagues that the manager would not like me having these, but I said, "If she had not been at the hair salon I would not have been put in that position." They obviously agreed with me and when I told my manager I now had a delivery pack in my car she did not say a word. She also never apologized for not being available when she was on call. Fortunately, everything turned out well but if the lady had run into problems it could have been another story.

Chapter 45
Normal Births After C-Sections

I was once called to a lady who was feeling unwell. It was a weekend and I had seen this lady at clinic several times and she really wanted to have a vaginal birth. Her first baby had been delivered by C-section because the baby had been in the breech position. I went to visit her and was reassured that she had a tummy bug. The baby was fine and I reassured her that she would start to feel better and not to worry about the baby being harmed by her vomiting.

Her mother was with her and brought up the question. What do you think about her having a water birth for this baby. I told her that at that time it was a rule at the hospital that women who had had a previous C-section could not deliver in the pool, but there was no reason why she couldn't have a vaginal birth. This was quite upsetting for the lady but I said to her, you could have a pool if you had a home birth. They looked pleased at that and I told them to discuss together with the husband decide what they wanted to do and I arranged to see her in the next antenatal clinic.

The lady arrived for her appointment and was happy to tell me that she wanted a home water birth. I told her that I would arrange this for her. I discussed it with the community manager and she said that if that is what the woman wanted, we would support her. I rang the woman who was delighted. I visited her when she was 36 weeks pregnant and made sure she was set up for her delivery and arranged to go on call for her myself.

The day of the delivery came and I arrived to find her in a good pattern of contractions. I examined her and she was already 6cm so we readied the pool and in she got. The lady wanted to have this baby without any pain relief, and she managed to do this because she was so relaxed. The time came to ring the second midwife and she went on to have a normal vaginal birth in the pool. It was lovely for her and for us as midwives, to be able to support her in her wishes.

After the delivery she was breast-feeding her baby and asked me if I would ring her mother. She gave me the number and I said, "That is the hospital number, does your mum work at the hospital."

"Yes," she told me, "she is on the Board of Directors." *Gulp I obviously didn't know that.*

Actually, I was really pleased as her mum would be able to tell those in high places how supportive the midwives were. It just shows that with the right support women can achieve their goals and it makes for a much better delivery for them with a happy mum and happy baby at the end of it. Who can ask for more than that.

I had another lady who had had her first two babies at a hospital in the North of the country and had recently moved into my area. She had had two C-sections and was desperate to have a vaginal birth. I went through her history with her. It turned out her first child had been in the breech position so she had had a C-section. Her second child was in the normal head down position but she had been advised to have a C-section as she had had one with her last baby. I explained to her that because she had a history of C-section she might be advised to have another C-section. I also told her that because she had not had a vaginal birth this would be a trial of labour; but as her last baby had been born over 2 years previously, there was no reason why she could not try for a vaginal birth.

I made this lady an appointment to see the consultant who also told her she could try for a vaginal birth. This was really good news for this lady and she was thrilled. I saw her throughout her pregnancy and she went into labour on one of my clinic days. I told her she was welcome to come to clinic and I would examine her, or I would see her at home at the end of my clinic. She opted to come to the surgery. All seemed to be well, her blood pressure was normal, the baby's heart beat was fine, and I examined her and she was already 5 cm which was really good news.

I advised her to go home and have some tea and make her way into the hospital. When the lady arrived on the delivery ward, it was thought by the staff because of her history that she would want a C-section. When she told the staff that this was not her wish they were quite surprised but very supportive. The outcome was she delivered vaginally less than an hour after she reached the hospital. Excellent news all round. I was proud of her for sticking to her guns.

On one of my visits, I went to see a lady whose baby was 10 days old, after a discussion it turned out the baby had not had its bowels open for about 7 days; the baby was well and breast-fed so it is not unusual for babies to go several days without pooing. I examined the baby and stripped it off ready to weigh it. When it was naked I lifted it up I told it, "You need to poo, your mummy is worried." Well guess what, the baby decided to poo right there and then. I was pebble dashed from top to toe.

It caused great hilarity and I told the baby that it had very good timing. I left a happy mum but had not the time to go home to change as I was due to start my clinic. I cleaned myself up as best I could with baby wipes and went off to antenatal clinic.

Half way through the clinic I visited the ladies and when I was washing my hands, I looked in the mirror and I noticed that my uniform tunic had several marks on it; in fact, it looked awful. I have some very polite ladies. I had seen several of the women and no one had said a word. I think they must have thought I had spilt my lunch down my top, 'Poor old girl she doesn't know where her mouth is.'

I remember with affection a lady I looked after who lived in a small village near where I lived. She had a little girl who had just started school and was pregnant with her 2nd child. Her pregnancy went well and she got to 37 weeks when she rang me and said she wasn't feeling the baby moving. I was at clinic so I asked her to come in and I would have a listen for her. Unfortunately, when she arrived I could not hear the heartbeat, so rang the hospital and she went off with her husband obviously very distressed. I rang the hospital after my clinic to hear the sad news that her baby had died and she was set to be induced the next day. It is so sad when someone loses a baby. As midwives we support these women to their best of our ability. I visited the lady in hospital the next day and saw her several times at home after she had delivered.

Two years later, I found out she was pregnant again and I was thrilled for her. Her pregnancy went well until 32 weeks when the baby went into distress. She was taken into theatre for an emergency C-section and I went with her. To our horror the baby did not breathe and, although, the doctors worked on him for what seemed an age, he could not be revived; so she had lost another baby. The atmosphere in theatre was tense and the poor lady was wailing in distress. It is something I will never forget. This lady needed a lot of support after she went home, I spent a lot of time with her but obviously she was beside herself with grief, as was her lovely husband.

The day of the funeral came and several of the midwives were in attendance; as I sat myself down, the vicar came up to me and asked me to read a poem. He handed it to me and disappeared. I was really apprehensive as it was a very moving poem and I was not used to speaking in public. I did get through the reading and then was extremely emotional. I could not fathom how this family were feeling and just wanted to scoop them up and protect them. It is an awful position to be in and all midwives want to support women with a healthy pregnancy, and to lose two babies is awful.

Chapter 46
More Home Births

I had a lady who wanted to have a home birth. She had had a normal first delivery and then had suffered three miscarriages. I told her there was no reason she should not have a home delivery but told her that I thought she should be seen by the consultant during her pregnancy because of her history. The Prof saw this lady and was happy for her to have a home birth. Fortunately, her pregnancy went very well and she got over the 37wks cut off for home births. The day of the delivery arrived, so I went to the house, she lived in a village at the far end of my area, so although it was fairly local to me it was 18miles from the hospital.

This lady lived in a beautiful house, she wanted to deliver in the bedroom which was very large and had a bath on a plinth adorning it. She spent some time in the bath, then was walking around and doing very well.

I called the 2nd midwife when she was 7cm as she had a way to come, and we waited for the baby to appear. After about an hour, she felt the urge to push and there was no sign of the 2nd midwife, so we just carried on. Twenty minutes later the lady delivered the baby and all was well. Still no 2nd midwife, who at that point rang me and said it was too far to come and she was going home.!!

I told the midwife that the lady had delivered and that I no longer needed her, she grumbled that I had called her out on for nothing. My reply if you had come when I asked you would have been here for the delivery. Well, I was told I was eating my supper.

It is beyond belief that a community midwife would do this, I know no other midwife who would dream of having their supper before answering a call. I suppose it takes all sorts to make the world go around but if anything had been amiss at the delivery I think she would have found herself in trouble with the management. I did tell the girls in the office what had happened and it did get back to management. The midwife was not happy and had the cheek to tell me off for telling people what had happened. She was actually a previous Manager so should really have known better.

I remember a lady who lived in a village who wanted a home delivery. She was having her 3rd baby and had had her previous babies in hospital. She had two girls and did not know what she was having this time.

Her pregnancy went well and eventually went into labour. I attended and all was going well, and she was relaxed and doing well. The time came for the 2nd midwife to be called and she came within twenty minutes, this lady went on to have a normal delivery of a beautiful baby boy. The parents were really happy with the birth and with their son and we left a very happy family behind us when we eventually left them. I saw her for her post-natal visits and all went very well.

I discharged this lady on the 10th day as all was well with both her and her baby. I saw this lady several weeks later when I was visiting another patient who was a friend of hers, and she burst into tears when she saw me. I thought something was wrong but she informed me that she was so happy with her delivery and her baby that she felt tearful every time she saw me. Bless her, it became a running joke. I bumped into her several times and it was always the same tears and a hug. It is so lovely when patients enjoy their births and feel really happy with all that happened.

Another lady I saw in my clinic, was a lady who had had 1 child and then had had 2 ectopic pregnancies, one on the left and one on the right fallopian tube. Both tubes had been removed at the time of the ectopic. No one knew how she got pregnant. It was a very unexpected but happy event for the couple as they thought their pregnancy days were over. I joked to her well you cannot have another ectopic pregnancy you have no tubes. Your husband has sperm that must be very athletic and jumped from the ovary to the uterus. It doesn't matter how she got pregnant she did, and the pregnancy went very well and she decided to have a home birth. I remember the delivery vividly. She was worried that because her first delivery had been difficult that she would not be able to cope. I reassured her that she would be much more relaxed at home and that we would be able to offer her pain relief if she needed it.

This lady went into labour on her due date which is actually quite unusual. She coped very well and went on to have a normal quick delivery and was very happy with this and her beautiful baby. We still do not know how she got pregnant. Usually ladies that have had both tubes removed need IVF to enable them to get pregnant. We will write this one up to don't know how it happened but so pleased for the couple that it did.

I remember well one Christmas day being on duty and getting a phone call from one of my ladies who was having contractions. I did not have equipment with me as l was not on call but made my way to her house. The woman was in early labour and was coping very well, so I arranged to go and do some more visits and for her to ring when she needed me.

The call came later that morning and back I went. The lady was now 7cm and doing very well, so I called the hospital and asked them to send a midwife out with the equipment. About an hour later the door knocker went and the husband went to the door to find a midwife scurrying back to her car after dumping the equipment on the doorstep. He brought the equipment in and I asked him where the midwife was. He told me what had happened so I went outside and asked the midwife as she was about to drive off, are you not coming in.

Her answer was, "I am not on call and I am going home for my lunch."

Well that went down well. The lady laboured well and delivered about 2pm. The husband said, "You must be hungry would you like some lunch."

"That would be lovely," was my reply, and I was handed a cheese sandwich.

I had delivered at a house where they were vegetarians and were having their Christmas dinner at the lady's parent's house. By the time I had left, gone back to the hospital with the equipment and finished all the paper work it was 7pm. I drove to my parent in laws' house and found my Christmas lunch ready and waiting for me. It was a very tiring but successful day.

Chapter 47
Phobias

Nausea in early pregnancy is very common and can be quite debilitating. I was asked by the GP to visit a lady of mine who had a phobia of being sick. This poor lady was having her first baby and when I visited her she was laying in her bed, refusing to get up as she was afraid she would be sick. I asked her if she was feeling sick, and she told me no but she knew if she got up she would be sick. This was a very difficult situation to deal with. I chatted to her about things she could do to help herself stop being sick such as wearing sea sickness bands or drinking ginger tea. She was having none of it. She was not going to move out of her bed until she reached three months of pregnancy. She was 6 weeks when I saw her. I talked to her about risks of staying in bed for such a long time, but she was having none of it. I said that the GP could give her a prescription for ante sickness medication if she wished. She said, "Well, I will have it but I am still not getting out of bed." I met her husband who was very supportive but obviously a bit frustrated with what was going on. He had stayed off work to look after her, but obviously could not stay at home for another 6wks. I discussed it with the GP who visited her and tried to persuade her to get up. The outcome of this was, she did not move from her bed for another 6wks until she got to 12wks of pregnancy. I did try to tell her not all women are sick, but to no avail. Sometimes you have to accept the inevitable and support the women and her husband as best you can. The husband did return to work and was obviously was very relieved when she reached her goal of 12wks.

I had another lady who was terrified of having a blood test. This poor girl was absolutely shaking at the thought of having a blood test. I talked her through what blood tests were needed and she knew she wanted to have them. Thankfully, she was with her husband who could support her, so I advised her it may be best if she lay down on the couch for the blood test to go ahead. She said to me just do it, well that was easier said than done. I tried to hide the syringe and needle from her but she just freaked out. She asked me just to do the test and not to listen to her.

I put the tourniquet on her arm and she started screaming. It was awful, I told her I could not do it with her screaming, "I feel as if I am abusing you."

"No, just do it," she told me.

I went to put the needle in her arm and she screamed like a banshee. Next thing is there was a knock at the door and the practice nurse came in to see if I was killing someone. Fortunately, with her help we managed to get the blood we needed. I don't know who was sweating the most, the lady, her husband or me. She told me after it was over she did not feel it and was happier than she had been about having the tests. My reply was, "Well, hopefully I will be on annual leave next time you are due a blood test." She was a lovely lady and we had a good laugh about it and guess what, the next blood test she took without a problem, good for her.

Poorly Ladies

One lady I looked after was extremely unwell after her delivery. She had delivered vaginally at a hospital in another area and was discharged on day 2. I remember very well visiting her the next day. I found her in bed, looking extremely unwell. She was pale, sweaty and I was worried straight away.

I asked her how she was feeling and she burst into tears. Poor thing, her stitches were extremely painful, and she was finding it difficult to have her bowels open. I examined her and was shocked. Her perineum, well I told her it looked like a monkey's backside. It was red extremely swollen and looked so painful. As I looked closer, I realised that her haemorrhoids had been stitched down to her perineum. She also was complaining of feeling breathless.

I called the GP and he came straight away. We had no option but to send her back into hospital. It turned out that she had had a pulmonary embolism (blood clot in her lungs). Her perineum had to be restructured and she was very poorly. I kept in contact with her family, and with her, and at one point her baby was sent home with the father as she was so ill.

It was a difficult situation and we supported the family as much as we could. This lady was in the hospital for three weeks and was sent home just before Christmas. She was still unwell and needed heparin (blood thinning injections) every day for a period of at least 6 weeks. This lady was so weak still and was having difficulty looking after her baby. She had the support of her lovely husband and parents who thankfully lived very close to her. She was obviously extremely traumatized about what had happened to her and needed a lot of support. Thankfully, after another lengthy stay in hospital she was sent home and gradually got better. This lady never had another baby and I am not surprised.

Chapter 48
Looking After Colleagues

I have looked after several colleagues who have been pregnant. One lady, I remember was having her first baby, she came for her booking appointment and told me she was a midwife but felt unable to practice as one because she liked everything to be normal and felt some hospitals intervened too much and too soon. I told her that I would treat her as a mother not a midwife, and she was very happy with this. She had an uneventful pregnancy and decided to have a home birth.

She had lots of worries that she would not be allowed to do this with her first baby. I reassured her that she could deliver where she wanted to as long as everything was normal. Her baby was in the breech position at 35 weeks, but, fortunately, the baby turned into the head down position so the home birth went ahead. This lady coped beautifully and eventually gave birth to a beautiful baby boy. She went on to have 2 more babies, both delivered at home by me, and did extremely well with all her pregnancies and births.

Another midwife I looked after, had 3 births at home. It is lovely to be able to look after these colleagues and to help them have their ideal birth. I feel it also helps them, especially, if they work as hospital midwives to make births as normal and homely as possible. I know that midwives who are pregnant have as much apprehension if not more than other ladies. They know what can go wrong, and sometimes they need a lot of reassurance, but that's what we are there for.

I remember visiting a lady in Newport Pagnell who was a midwife. I had never met her before but was covering for a colleague who was on a day off. I did not get to this lady until late afternoon, and it was the weekend. When I arrived, she was sitting very gingerly and was very uncomfortable with her stitches. I went upstairs with her as she had several visitors and examined her abdomen, and then asked her if she would mind me looking at her stitches. Well, she said, "Nobody else has offered, but yes please do." Her perineum was extremely swollen and broken down and obviously infected.

"Right," I said, "this is what we are going to do; the surgery is closed, I am going to ring Labour ward." I rang them and they kindly saw her and gave her the antibiotics she needed.

I am shocked that no other midwife had observed her stitches. We always ask the women for their permission, and if they decline that's fine but midwives need as much care as anyone else, and in this case this young midwife was extremely grateful.

One of my colleagues from the district nursing team was pregnant and was wanting a home birth. This was her second baby and there was no medical or obstetric reason why this would be a problem. She had a normal pregnancy and eventually went into labour. Fortunately, I was able to attend and it was a fun delivery. I have never seen before or since what this lady was doing to get herself through her contractions. She marched on the spot for hours, it was hilarious and we teased her endlessly about it; she smiled and marched all night until it was time to deliver. A beautiful baby boy was the outcome and everything was normal. This lady was so relaxed it was wonderful to watch, I so admired her, I was a wreck when I was in labour. We often laughed about her marching when she returned to work and I told her she should do her midwifery, she would make a good midwife but she was happy in her job so that did not happen.

Names

I remember well, visiting a lady in a village on day 5 which is when the baby's blood test is due. I had not met this lady before as she was a colleague's patient. We got around to filling the form in for the baby's blood test, and she told me she was calling the baby Luke. "That's a lovely name," said I, "and what will the baby's surname be?" I asked as I knew she was not married.

"Warm," she told me.

Immediately, I said, "Luke Warm?"

"Yes," she said, "I do hope this baby was not called Tepid the rest of his life."

I have also had other amusing names, Theresa Green, Annette Curtains, the list goes on; I do wish women could look forward in time when labelling their babies with "different" names. Bo Bo Bailey was one I remember with humour, it's a great name for a baby, but for a teenager could cause problems I would have thought.

When babies are born parents have six weeks to register their baby. Most ladies do this quite soon after the birth, but I know one lady who left it until the last minute. The law says that if a baby is not registered by six weeks they can be fined; I don't know if this has ever happened.

Mums Who Read Baby Books

I am all for reading up on how you can help yourself to give birth, or how to look after your baby. Some women take it to extremes. I was sitting in the office one morning when a lady rang and asked to speak to the midwife who was visiting her. I went to the phone and the lady informed me that I could visit at ten past ten when the baby would be awake for thirty minutes to enable me to perform the heel prick on the baby. I said I would try but it was really difficult to give an exact time. I was told that she was following a plan in a book which was extremely regimented and if I was later than the allotted time I would not be allowed to do the test. Well, I managed to arrive at the house with five minutes to spare. I was told I would have to do the test in the baby's nursery, as the lights had to be kept down according to the manual.

Well, doing a blood test in the dark is not the easiest of things to do, but at ten to ten we went upstairs; I washed my hands and picked up the baby, and managed to perform the blood test. I then weighed the baby and the mother then took the baby from me, put it in the cot and we left the room with the baby crying. When I talked to the mother about the regime, she told me that she wanted to keep to a schedule and expected the baby to do as the book said. I talked to her about all her worries and told her that although she wanted the baby to keep to the manual, the baby had not read the book so did not know what it was supposed to do. Fortunately, her husband agreed with me, and I told her to just enjoy her baby, and go with the flow. According to the schedule, the baby only saw daylight for 2 hours a day, and the rest of the time it was expected to sleep. This is unrealistic for a baby, and also very stressful for the parents. I left them to chat about their expectations, and not to expect too much of themselves. I gave them my phone number and told them to ring me if they had any questions.

Later that day, I had a phone call from the husband who told me he had thrown the book in the bin. His wife agreed with him that what they were trying to do was unrealistic, and unworkable. It is so sad when ladies expect too much of themselves or their babies. Just enjoy them, babyhood it doesn't last for long and it is so important to be relaxed around them, otherwise, babies pick up on it and are more unsettled. I spoke to the lady a few days later, and she told me that the baby was in quite a good routine and that she and her husband were much less stressed.

"Excellent, that's what I like to hear."

Chapter 49
Shoulder Dystocia

Shoulder dystocia means that the baby's head is delivered and then the shoulders get stuck, it is a medical emergency and at the hospital from which I worked we had training every year on medical emergencies.

I was asked to attend as second midwife to a lady having her fifth baby. The first midwife was new to community and so I was happy to attend. The midwife was very pleased to see me and the lady was doing well. She decided she wanted to deliver on all fours, in her bathroom. This was fine but there was not a lot of space. I had an area outside the bathroom ready, with oxygen and suction, in case the baby needed any help so we were set for the delivery. The lady had had four babies before with no problems so we were not expecting this delivery to be any different. How wrong we were. The lady got to 10cm and duly started to push. I was standing to one side when I picked up that the midwife was having a problem delivering the baby's shoulders. After a long minute the midwife said, "I cannot do it," and so asked me to take over. Fortunately, with a few movements, I managed to deliver the baby who, as expected, was very shocked and needed help. The first midwife was in shock, so I took the baby to attend to it, and asked her to stay with the lady and to phone for an ambulance.

I managed to get the baby to breathe but it was clear that it needed to be transferred into hospital as it was grunting. (A sign that the baby is not happy.) The other midwife had called for an ambulance and had delivered the placenta, so I updated the parents about the baby. Who by this time was breathing normally but still flaring its nose (a sign of distress). The parents were obviously shocked but understood what was happening.

The ambulance arrived and the lady and her baby were taken to hospital with the first midwife accompanying them. I cleared up and followed in my car. When I arrived on delivery ward, the baby had been seen by a paediatrician and was being admitted to the special care baby unit. The mother was, fortunately, well and was relieved that her baby would eventually be fine.

The first midwife was in shock and was being comforted by the delivery ward sister. I went along to join them and reassured her that everything was fine and that's why we had two midwives at deliveries; so that we could support each other. It turned out that this had been her first home birth since she had finished her training. I felt so sorry for her, she was a really good midwife and had had an unfortunate start to her community career. We had several long chats about what had happened, and she eventually began to feel better. I think if that had been my first delivery as a new midwife I would have felt exactly the same and she did well to regain her confidence. Good for her.

I had seen a lot of shoulder dystocia before but normally they happened in hospital, so it was a rare thing for it to happen on community, especially with a fifth baby, but it can happen at any time and that's why midwives are trained so well in such things. There are certain things that can be done to help the lady deliver a baby who is stuck but it is quite different on community, especially when stuck in a small space; so you learn to improvise and this comes with experience. On the delivery ward, you press the bell for help and the world comes running, midwives, doctors and anyone else who is about. This is one reason I feel that any midwife who works on community should want to be there, not just forced to do it as part of her career pathway. Recently, we have had midwifes who have been sent out to work on community when they really did not want to be there. I say each to his own, I love community but not everyone does. Managers need to take into account each midwives preference and where they feel most comfortable. This does not always happen. I also feel it makes the ladies experience more fragmented as these midwives were only coming out to community for a short period of time.

Chapter 50
Unusual Events

One of my ladies rang me after I had had a weekend off and asked me if I could visit as she was feeling a lot of pain in her perineum. I went as she had asked and found her to be sitting very gingerly on the sofa. We went up to her bedroom to see what the problem was and I was quite shocked. She had not had any stitches but was extremely swollen around her labial area. She had what is called a haematoma on her labia, which is a collection of blood. It looked extremely painful and very sore. I phoned the ladies GP who asked me to ring the delivery ward. I duly rang them and the lady was admitted to hospital, she was later taken to theatre to have the blood drained, which made her feel a lot more comfortable. Her baby had been admitted with her so she spent the next day in hospital so that she could recover. The lady came home the next day and felt a lot more comfortable but it took a few days for her to feel better. She wondered why this had not been picked up earlier, but as I told her as she had not had any stitches although we would ask her how she felt we would not necessarily look unless we worried that there was a problem. Fortunately, this lady recovered very well and had no further problems.

I remember with humour a lady who I delivered one night in the maternity unit. She was a Chinese lady whose husband was with her. She was having her first baby and was coping really well during her contractions. It was quite a long time before she was ready to deliver and her husband was complaining quite vocally that he was tired. Actually, so was I, I had worked all day and had been called into the unit to help as they were short staffed. Eventually, I put a mattress on the floor for him and told him to put his head down, and I would wake him when the baby was ready to be born. He readily agreed with this, and quickly went to sleep. The lady eventually had the urge to push and so I tried to wake the husband. That was more difficult that it sounds, he was fast asleep and after a while I said to the lady I am going to wash my hands ready to deliver your baby, she was upset that her husband was fast asleep; so I washed my hands, put my gloves on and as I helped her I was prodding him with my foot. Eventually, he roused, his first words were, I am still tired.

That did not go down very well, and his wife just told him to suck it up and come and hold her hand. He did rouse and did hold her hand, but as soon as she had delivered her baby daughter, he told her in no uncertain terms that he was going home as he had had a long day. I must admit, I was slightly shocked but she took it with good grace and told me that if he did not get enough sleep, he was grumpy. Poor thing, fortunately, after taking this lady and her baby to the ward I was able to go home and get into my own bed.

Diabetes in pregnancy seems to be increasing these days, whether this is due to weight, lifestyle or ethnicity. At 28wks of pregnancy lots of ladies are now tested for diabetes. Diabetes can cause a lot of problems in pregnancy with babies being more likely to have problems with or after the birth. Blood sugars can be a problem for these babies, and they are more likely to be big but are not big healthy babies. Ladies with type one diabetes who take insulin need to be very closely followed during their pregnancies, but now with a lot of ladies who are being diagnosed with type 2 diabetes are also falling into this category.

These ladies all need to be under consultant care and a lot of them need to be induced before their due date. They are more likely to have intervention in their deliveries and the babies are more likely to be admitted to the special care baby unit. This is a huge problem for maternity services. A specialist diabetic midwife was assigned at my hospital and she was very busy.

A lady I remember coming to clinic was found to have a lot of sugar in her urine. I took her blood sugar which showed she was in the higher limit of normal. I talked to her about her diet, did she have sugar in her drinks, did she eat a lot of processed food etc. The answer to everything was, "No, I eat a very healthy diet, I cook everything from scratch."

So, I made an appointment for her to have a fasting blood sugar test, this meant she had to eat nothing after 10pm and then just water until she had her blood test. As I did afternoon clinics, I made this appointment with the practice nurses.

Later that afternoon, I had a phone call from her telling me she had been thinking about her diet, and did I think that the 2-litre bottle of lemonade that she drank every day could be causing a problem. I think we may have found the culprit. I saw this lady two weeks later and, behold, she had no sugar in her urine and her fasting blood sugar was normal. We did have a laugh about her lemonade habit. She told me she had not had any since I told her about it. Good for her, she went on to have a beautiful baby girl, but she told me she had taken a bottle of lemonade into the ward to drink after the baby had been born.

Most expectant mothers are very good about their diet, but there are some who see it as a way to eat more. I had one lady who was thrilled to be pregnant and when I talked through diet with her, her face dropped. "Oh," she said, "I was hoping I could eat what I liked." I gave her lots of leaflets with information of what was best to eat in pregnancy and off she went.

When I saw her later on in her pregnancy, she was worried about the weight she had put on since she had been pregnant. She was now 15wks pregnant and had put on two stones. I talked to her about her diet, and she told me she had a craving for fried chicken from a certain shop, she was eating it most days of the week. This came with chips, fizzy drinks and was costing her a fortune. I gave her advice on trying to change this habit. Fortunately for her and her baby, she went on to put very little weight on in the rest of her pregnancy as she started cooking properly and thus, ate well.

Early on in my community life, I remember visiting a lady who had delivered her first baby. She was being helped by her mother, who when I entered the house was holding the baby. The baby was 7 days old, and the mother was worried because the baby had been vomiting. As I got nearer to the mother, I noticed that she was feeding the baby rice pudding straight out of a tin. I was extremely shocked and explained to the girl and her mother that the baby could not digest this and it would make the baby ill. The girl's mother informed me that she had done the same for her children and it had done them no harm, and it helped them sleep. I was so worried that I went to see the ladies GP and Health Visitor. They both informed me that they knew this family well, and would advise them not to do this, but they didn't think this would make any difference; but they would keep a close eye on the baby. We are there to give advice. The upbringing of the baby is up to the parents. This lady's mother went home shortly after this event, fortunately, the girl went back to feeding her baby with a bottle of milk.

Chapter 51
Retirement

The day and the time had come for me to retire. I have worked as a midwife for 45 years and had a really fulfilling career. I loved all my ladies and their babies. I knew that was something I would miss, but I wanted to retire before I became too old and made a mistake. I have delivered over two thousand babies and can look back with fondness at my career.

The year before I retired my eldest daughter Charlotte, had got a teaching job in the local school in the area where I practiced. When she first started and when to meet the parents, there was a lot of whispering about her name. She had to tell them that she was my daughter; I had delivered the babies she, would teach them. What a wonderful legacy, it is always lovely to talk to Charlotte about all the children in her class and how well they are doing. I am one proud mother.

I had one lady who had booked for a home birth and I spoke to my manager and arranged that I would deliver her even after my retirement day. This lady eventually started contracting and off I trotted. The lady was in established labour. She had her husband and her mother with her. A lot of the night was spent in and out of the pool, but this baby had a mind of its own. I called the second midwife when she was eight centimetres hoping that the baby would put in an appearance. Several hours later, it was evident that this baby was not going to oblige and we had to make a decision to transfer into the hospital.

An ambulance was called and we all transferred into the hospital. I left the lady in the care of the staff on delivery ward and was driven back the house to get my car. I was extremely pleased to get home but a bit disappointed that I had not managed to deliver this ladies baby. The lady went on to have a normal birth a few hours later and was happy with all the care she had received. I saw her some weeks later and her baby was lovely.

The hospital gave me a good send off. I had an evening out at a local Chinese restaurant, a last day breakfast and a wonderful voucher to spend at my favourite shop. At my final clinic, I had so many bouquets of flowers I had a job getting into my car.

The surgery also did me proud, I went out with all the girls for a meal. I was presented me with theatre vouchers and flowers. The doctors very kindly took me out for a meal and presented me with a beautiful dish with all their names on it. They also gave me a gift of an afternoon tea for two, which Richard and I really enjoyed. I also had over seventy-five cards. I was overwhelmed with all the kindness.

I had been retired a fortnight when I got a phone call asking me to do some bank shifts. I did do some for the following few months, but then I decided to stop altogether.

I do miss all my mums and their babies, but when I have Evee on a Wednesday, I take her to pre-school and catch up with some of them. I am still being contacted by some of my ladies who need help. One of these ladies had a word with my daughter as she was expecting twins and wanted to be delivered in a Unit other than the one I had been attached to.

Ladies can deliver where they like and, although this is an easy process, nobody wanted to do it for her. In the end, I asked her to go into the surgery and get all the forms and I went to her house and filled them out for her. Her own midwife had been on annual leave so was obviously not happy that her colleagues had not done this for the lady. It is easy to fulfil the wishes of ladies and causes a lot of stress for them when they have to fight for what they want.

I heard later this lady had been to the hospital of her choice and they were not happy that she had not been transferred to them earlier. All this could have been done much earlier on in her pregnancy just by filling out a form. I find it very frustrating, but midwives are being given more and more to do so I don't blame them for not wanting to fill out yet another form.

As a retired midwife, I at first found it really difficult to leave all the ladies I thought of as mine. Times are changing, midwives now have an awful lot of pressure put onto them, this comes from managers, the hospital hierarchy and sometimes my feeling is that the ladies get lost and blur into the background. Hospitals are so busy these days, the birth rate is rising, and the paperwork that is beyond comprehension. Midwives are looking after women with complicated pregnancies, this comes with more appointments, scans and consultant appointments. In the end, all midwives go into the profession to help women have a normal pregnancy with a beautiful baby at the end of it. Ladies' expectations are rising, they know their rights which is great but can lead to disappointment.

I was lucky enough to work with a great bunch of midwives, they worked hard but sometimes you could feel their frustrations, when things seemed to change just for the sake of it. I always put my ladies first and sometimes that did not go down very well with management. The best thing about ladies being given choices is they feel empowered and this leads to them having a happy pregnancy with a great outcome. I know my ladies appreciated me, and in return they gave me a lot of pleasure. I know that I picked the right profession for me. I have had a great career and brought over two thousand babies into the world. Who could ask for more.